MW01102312

Stewart's

QUOTABLE AFRICAN WOMEN

Other books by Julia Stewart:

Stewart's Quotable Africa (Penguin, 2004)
Words to the Wise: A Collection of African Proverbs
(Spearhead, 2003)
*Rwanda Recovery: UNHCR's Repatriation and
Reintegration Activities in Rwanda from 1994-1999*
(UNHCR, 2000)
*Eccentric Graces: Eritrea and Ethiopia Through the Eyes
of a Traveler* (Red Sea Press, 1999)
African Proverbs and Wisdom (Carol Publishing, 1997)
*The African-American Book of Days: Inspirational
History and Thoughts for Every Day of the Year* (Carol
Publishing, 1996)
1,001 African Names (Carol Publishing, 1996)
African Names (Carol Publishing, 1993)

Stewart's

QUOTABLE AFRICAN WOMEN

Julia Stewart

PENGUIN BOOKS

PENGUIN BOOKS

Published by the Penguin Group
Penguin Books Ltd, 80 Strand, London WC2R 0RL, England
Penguin Group (USA) Inc, 375 Hudson Street, New York, New York
10014, USA
Penguin Group (Canada), 90 Eglinton Avenue East, Suite 700, Toronto,
Ontario, Canada M4P 2Y3 (a division of Pearson Penguin Canada Inc)
Penguin Ireland, 25 St Stephen's Green, Dublin 2, Ireland
(a division of Penguin Books Ltd)
Penguin Group (Australia), 250 Camberwell Road, Camberwell, Victoria
3124, Australia (a division of Pearson Australia Group Pty Ltd)
Penguin Books India Pvt Ltd, 11 Community Centre, Panchsheel Park,
New Delhi – 110 017, India
Penguin Group (NZ), Cnr Rosedale and Airborne Roads, Albany,
Auckland 1310, New Zealand (a division of Pearson New Zealand Ltd)
Penguin Books (South Africa) (Pty) Ltd, 24 Sturdee Avenue, Rosebank,
Johannesburg 2196, South Africa

Penguin Books (South Africa) (Pty) Ltd, Registered Offices:
24 Sturdee Avenue, Rosebank, Johannesburg 2196, South Africa

www.penguinbooks.co.za

First published by Penguin Books (South Africa) (Pty) Ltd 2005

ISBN 0 143 02486 8

Typeset by CJH Design in 10/12.5pt Oranda
Cover design: African Icons
Printed and bound by CTP Book Printers, Cape Town

*Our problem is that we have listened so rarely to women's
voices,
the noises of men having drowned us out . . .*

Adeola James, in her introduction to *In Their Own Voices:
African Women Writers Talk*, 1990, p2

This book is dedicated to Olive Schreiner,

*fittingly in the year which is the 150th anniversary of
her birth – the African woman who, by many twists of
fate, now provides me with shelter and new ways of
understanding, as well as questioning*

and

to all African women;

LISTEN TO THEM

Table of Contents

Author's Note

It seems to me that there is always this silencing of the African woman's voice.
And as I get older, I am very sad to see that there is no one to protect us or fight for us. We are very alone.
Kola Boof

I sit before my computer wholly ashamed. *Stewart's Quotable Africa* was published in 2004 by Penguin Books, a groundbreaking work, if I say so myself, a book that illustrated the breadth and depth of African writing and thought. The long-overdue 'Bartlett's of Africa', with over 5000 quotes by Africans or about Africa, selected by a competent woman writer and editor with appropriate training and years of African experience. So when Penguin South Africa's publisher Jeremy Boraine asked me to put together a shorter version with just quotes from African women, I thought: No problem, easy job. Just extract the women's quotes from *Stewart's Quotable Africa* and there you'll have the smaller women's book, with the 750 requested quotes.

To my horror I found that when I extracted the women speakers from *Stewart's Quotable Africa*, there were only 400 quotes! Less than one-tenth of the quotes I'd gathered were from African women.

So I set to work to right my wrong, and this book is the result. I hope it will help make up for my having committed what is one of the most persistent crimes against women – overlooking them, in a world that is crying for their healing voices.

Good often comes of our errors. In my search for quotes from African women, I discovered (to me) fresh and inspiring talent. I am thrilled to have been introduced through this task to some African women who are blowing all the old rules right out of the water. A few spring to mind: Unity Dow, Botswana's first female High Court judge; Kenyan Professor Wangari Maathai, an environmentalist and the first African woman to be awarded the Nobel Peace Prize; Antjie Krog, a South African poet and writer whose works are helping an entire country wrap its mind around a new identity.

There are the Nigerian poets, like Lola Shoneyin and Chika Unigwe, who speak with a disarming frankness and honesty, and who use their voices to promote social responsibility and women's advancement. There is Cameroonian novelist Calixthe Beyala whose despair at Africa's poverty and whose struggles with sexism and exile are shared by many. Marianne Thamm's lexis shows up in force, because this South African columnist has something witty to say on just about everything. And don't forget to pay close attention to writer Kola Boof, the firebrand from the Sudan. Her words pack as much punch as her name.

Egyptian feminist and doctor Nawal El Saadawi and a host of Algerian women speak with candid tongues under repressive – even life-threatening – conditions. They remind us that in the 21st century millions of women throughout the world remain violently repressed, their valuable labour lost, their healing voices silenced.

I have also come across FEMRITE, an organisation founded by Ugandan women writers to support women's writing and publishing. FEMRITE is 'determined to turn Uganda's literary desert into a haven for women's voices'. FEMRITE is an exciting initiative, and I hope there will be more of this type of self-support for African women's voices.

As I live in Olive Schreiner's house and her books surround me, I have felt it fitting to resuscitate her prophetic voice from the Victorian era, for much of what she said then – as women's rights activist, peace campaigner, and general champion of the underdog – is valid today. Another revived pioneering woman of South Africa is Elsa Smithers. The obscure Smithers reminds us that many 'ordinary' women are leading truly extraordinary lives, and if they can find time and means to fix it on paper, they can be excellent witnesses to their times.

Women have not only been witnesses to, but also actors and key players in their times. However, while there have been many women in African governments, the number occupying the highest echelons can be counted on one hand. The first and only woman to head a modern African state was Ruth Perry of Liberia, serving as interim Head of State from 1996-1997. Only three women have been Prime Ministers in Africa: Elizabeth Domitien (Central African Republic), Agathe Uwilingiyimana (Rwanda), and Sylvie Kinigi (Burundi). Men have dominated Africa in terms of leadership and politics, and arguably this could be seen as one arena in which Africa has been failing. Women in this book have their say about these topics; most think they could do better, and believe that women must make a greater effort to rise to the task.

I hope that what has been created with this collection of quotes is an entrance into new worlds, new perspectives, from women of Africa, from all walks of life. Their thoughts may cover wide-ranging subjects, and represent varying opinions, but as you read, it begins to sound as if there is one voice, that grows louder and louder. The voice of reason, the voice of perseverance, the voice of women.

Julia Stewart
Hanover, Northern Cape, South Africa
February 2005

Subject Index

Ability

There's really no line between able-bodied and disabled swimming ... I treat both of them the same. They're your opponents and you've got to race the way you train. It is important to swim your own race and not someone else's.

Natalie du Toit, South African Paralympic gold medallist in swimming, 'Natalie du Toit: Ability of Mind', 16 September 2004 (www.southafrica.info/women)

I know that my guts will drip across the American landscape like acid and good sex and sunshine. Like Aretha Franklin can sing, I too, am gifted.

Kola Boof, Sudanese-American writer and activist, interview with Jennifer Williams, 'The Africana QA: Kola Boof', 18 May 2004 (Africana website)

If we have intelligence, imagination, and the ability to dream, things can happen.

Graça Machel, Mozambican educator and politician, interview with Vukani Magubane, 'Graça Machel on Her Work, Her Grief, and Her Love for Nelson Mandela', *Ebony*, May 1997, p162

The love of beauty and the desire for it must be born in a man; the skill to reproduce it he must make.

Olive Schreiner, South African writer, *The Story of an African Farm*, 1883 (Penguin, 1995, p170)

Action and Activism

Fear no one, speak up.

> Self-proclaimed mantra of **Patricia de Lille**, South African
> politician (*Great South Africans*, 2004, p97)

In order to make things change and evolve, you need
to get up and take action.

> **Nahawa Doumbia**, Malian singer, interview with Kristell
> Diallo, March 2001, New York (Afropop Worldwide)

I want to go and come. And not be there standing
still while the world around me is in rapid motion.
I too want to move ... move with my eyes! The
principle of life is to give and take! Let me 'give'; let
me 'take' from the world around me.

> Excerpt from 'Tell It to Women', 1997, by Nigerian playwright
> **Tess Onsonye Onwueme**

We must make our choice or others, less sympathetic, will make that choice for us.

> **Wangari Maathai**, Kenyan environmental and human rights
> activist, 'Bottle-Necks of Development in Africa', paper
> presented at the 4th UN World Women's Conference in
> Beijing, China, August-September 1995

I hate bullies. I stand for simple justice, equal
opportunity and human rights. The indispensable
elements in a democratic society – and well worth
fighting for.

> **Helen Suzman**, South African parliamentarian (The Helen
> Suzman Foundation website)

Once I had absorbed the ill-treatment that blacks were subjected to, which happened quite early in my life, I thought that you can't stay in this country unless you do something about it.

Helen Suzman, South African parliamentarian, 1995 interview, *Cutting Through the Mountain*, p423

I married a commitment to improve the lives of my people. I have not divorced this commitment and it has not divorced me either.

Winnie Madikizela-Mandela, South African politician and former wife of Nelson Mandela, speaking at the American University in Washington, DC (*The Citizen* (South Africa), 17 April 1996, p12)

When you deal with movements at the grass-roots level you are confronted with poverty, under-development. You ask, 'Why do some people live in misery? Does it have to be like this?' and you realize that some people who present themselves as the friends of the people are really the enemies of the people. You can't just keep planting trees. You begin to plant a few ideas. When you confront them, that is when you are called subversive.

Wangari Maathi, Kenyan environmental and human rights activist (Lucy Komisar, *Baltimore Sun*, early 1990s)

If you won't conform to society you must always fight it. No rest.

Olive Schreiner, South African writer, in a letter dated February 1890 (Beeton, p70)

Africa

Africa … despite its current difficulties, remains
the continent of all possibilities for the whole of
humanity.

> **Werewere Liking**, Cameroonian playwright, interview with
> Michelle Mielly, Ki-Yi Village, Abidjan, Côte d'Ivoire, 2 June
> 2002 (African Postcolonial Literature in the Postcolonial Web)

Africa is never out of fashion.

> **Mahen Bonetti**, cinema curator from Sierra Leone,
> 'Reclaiming Honor; African Film Fest Hopes to Challenge
> Perceptions', interview with Jacque Lynn Schiller, *indieWire.
> com*, 5 April 2002

While we may be thinking of leaving Africa, Africa
may very well leave us.

> South African playwright **Fiona Coyne**, from her play *As the
> Koekie Crumbles*, 1999

What is the future of this dying continent? It is a
people that makes me ashamed because we are
the only ones in the world who are not able to free
ourselves. Africa is crazy. Everyone is crazy there.
Whenever I go to Africa, I myself become a bit crazy.
I cannot live in Africa.

> **Calixthe Beyala**, Cameroonian novelist, 1996 interview
> with Emmanuel Matateyou (Ayo Abiétou Coly, 'Neither Here
> nor There: Calixthe Beyala's Collapsing Homes', *Research in
> African Literatures*, Volume 33, Number 2) (iupjournals.org)

Africa has her mysteries, and even a wise man cannot understand them. But a wise man respects them.

Miriam Makeba, South African singer and civil rights activist, *Makeba, My Story*, 1988, p243

That is not a place to visit unless one chooses to be an exile ever afterwards from an inexplicable majestic silence lying just over the border of memory or of thought. Africa gives you the knowledge that man is a small creature, among other creatures, in a larger landscape.
Doris Lessing, English-Zimbabwean author, *African Stories*, 1981, preface

Teach me to laugh once more
let me laugh with Africa my mother
I want to dance to her drum-beats
I am tired of her cries
Grace Akello, Ugandan poet, 'Encounter,' *My Barren Song*, 1980 (Busby, p638)

Has God forgotten that he ever created Africa? … kindle my powers of reason so that I do not look at this continent with only fear in my heart.
Sheila Fugard, South African novelist and poet, *The Castaways*, 1972 (2002 edition, p18)

There are as many Africas as there are books about Africa.
Beryl Markham, English-born East African aviator, *West With the Night*, 1942 (Penguin, 1988 edition, p7)

Africa is less a wilderness than a repository of primary and fundamental values, and less a barbaric land than an unfamiliar voice.

Beryl Markham, English-born East African aviator, *West With the Night*, 1942 (Penguin, 1988 edition, p239)

I wish you could go once to my old African world and know what it is to stand quite alone on a mountain in the still, blazing sunshine, and the clear, clear blue above you, and the great unbroken plains stretching away as far as you can see, without a trace of the human creature, perhaps not a living creature higher in the scale than an ant within miles and miles of you! I always wish you could be there, then you would know how the *One* God was invented.

Olive Schreiner, South African writer, in a letter to Karl Pearson, 16 June 1886 (Beeton, p106)

Africans

... everyone had their own take or prognosis on what Africa and African was. I felt here again, someone else is speaking for us. Where is our own voice in this discourse?

Mahen Bonetti, cinema curator from Sierra Leone, 'Reclaiming Honor; African Film Fest Hopes to Challenge Perceptions', interview with Jacque Lynn Schiller, *indieWire. com*, 5 April 2002

Sobukwe's belief that an African was anyone who gave allegiance to Africa, regardless of their skin colour, resonated with me. It gave me an identity and a home.

Patricia de Lille, South African politician, from her biography *Patricia de Lille* written by journalist Charlene Smith (www. safrica.info)

My soul is African. It is from there that springs the fountain of my creative being.

Tsitsi Dangarembga, Zimbabwean writer (www.kirjasto.sci. fi/tsitsi.htm)

A people less endowed with the power of the human spirit would have become extinct and wiped from the face of this planet.

Wangari Maathai, Kenyan environmental and human rights activist, 'Bottle-Necks of Development in Africa', paper presented at the 4th UN World Women's Conference in Beijing, China, August-September 1995

Afrikaners

As long as the Afrikaner keeps hanging on to a single view of history, we'll remain pillars of salt like Lot's wife. Anyway, we must learn to look ahead, not backwards!

Dalene Matthee, South African novelist, *The Day the Swallows Spoke*, 1992, p31

My Oupa swore that the English potteries cast their cups with saucers attached so they didn't have to listen to Boers slurping their coffee.

Zoë Wicomb, South African writer, 'A Trip to the Gifberge', 1987 (Medalie, p120)

The Dutch were quick with their guns, and hard to like as it is to like the Caffres, and loving their land and their possessions, my being a man only an accident, even though the Dutch spoke about God, a cruel God that sent people who were dark of skin into an even darker darkness.
   Sheila Fugard, South African novelist and poet, *The Castaways*, 1972 (2002 edition, p6)

It is usually a dreary business, visiting the old-fashioned Dutch farmer in his home, though one cannot accuse him of a lack of hospitality. There is no pretence at beauty in or outside the house, and a flower-garden is practically unknown ... Conversation is stilted and confines itself to inquiries about mealie crops and live stock. During this time the housewife is mostly out of the room preparing indifferent coffee or placing pieces of dried apricot roll ... on a dish, to hand round to her visitors.
   Elsa Smithers, South African farmer, *March Hare*, 1935, p202

The Bantu and the Englishman may be found elsewhere on the earth's surface in equal or greater perfection; but the Boer, like our plumbagos, our silvertrees, and our kudus, is peculiar to South Africa.
   Olive Schreiner, South African writer, *Thoughts on South Africa*, 1923 (1992 edition, p60)

I learnt that in the African Boer we have one of the most intellectually virile and dominant races the world has seen; a people who beneath a calm and almost stolid surface hide the intensest passions and the most indomitable resolutions.

Olive Schreiner, South African writer (Emslie, p xiii)

Yet it is not so much their freeing [black slaves] which drove us to such lengths, as their being placed on equal footing with Christians, contrary to the laws of God, and the natural distinctions of race and colour, so that it was intolerable for any decent Christian to bow down beneath such a yoke; wherefore we rather withdraw in order to preserve our doctrines of purity.

Anna Steenkamp, a Voortrekker, explaining in her memoirs why her people left the Cape after the British ended slavery there (www.whoosh.org/issue35)

Age and Ageing

I grew older and more blasé.

South African writer and journalist **Marianne Thamm**, column on celebrities entitled 'Flashes in the pan', 18 July 2001 (*Mental Floss*, 2002, p29)

At my age, I don't want to do things I'm supposed to. I will do the things I want to.

Graça Machel, Mozambican educator and politician, 'Graça Machel on Her Work, Her Grief, and Her Love for Nelson Mandela', by Vukani Magubane, *Ebony*, May 1997, p162

'Age ain't nothin' but a number.' But age is other things, too. It is wisdom, if one has lived one's life properly. It is experience and knowledge. And it is getting to know all the ways the world turns, so that if you cannot turn the world the way you want, you can at least get out of the way so you won't get run over.

    Miriam Makeba, South African singer and civil rights activist, *Makeba, My Story*, 1988, p201

I am not old and ugly yet but you can see your death in my changing face.

    Nadine Gordimer, South African writer, 'Time Did', *A Soldier's Embrace*, 1975 (1983 edition, p53)

In her youth her eyes had been beautiful, but there was none who now remembered her youth and in old age she looked out upon the world with a patient endurance which had in it something of the strength and something of the melancholy of the labouring ox.

    Pauline Smith, South African writer, 'Desolation' (Dodd, p45)

Now, being old, I cannot work quite so hard and must confess that for the first time I know what it means to feel a little dull. They say that time passes quickly when you are old, but it is not true. It seems to me that in youth and even in middle age the hours flash by, but that in old age time often goes on leaden wheels.

    Elsa Smithers, South African farmer, *March Hare*, 1935, p1

Sometimes years pass … and we feel they are years of decay, we are growing old; and we feel a kind of despair; then of God cometh not with observation. Sometimes while we are regretting that our branches do not blossom; then is a great store of sap silently rising and forming, which will cover them with blossoms, afterwards – one day.

Olive Schreiner, South African writer, in a letter to Karl Pearson, 11 November 1885 (Beeton, p95)

Alcohol

I believe in the redeeming power of margheritas, especially two or three margheritas.

Diane Awerbuck, South African writer, *Gardening at Night*, 2003, p4

When I'm out with my mates I love to get legless.

Samantha Mumba, Zambian-Irish pop star, interview with Paul Martin, *ShowBiz Ireland* news, 11 January 2002

When Sowetans throw parties, they mean business. Starting on Friday night and known as stokvels, they go on through Saturday, Sunday and often Monday. Guests pay dearly for the entertainment, emerging after three wild days with what they call TB – terrible bhabhalazi (hangovers) – and empty pockets.

Heidi Holland, South African journalist and writer, *Born in Soweto*, 1995, Chapter 9

The emaciated ditch-digger weeps sometimes as he digs. It is on Mondays that the sight occurs among them, when he is suffering from the drink their religion forbids.

Nadine Gordimer, South African writer, 'For Dear Life', *A Soldier's Embrace*, 1975 (1983 edition, p71)

Alienation

Since the day I was born I have been an exile. I felt alienated from my own body and from everything around me.

Nawal El Saadawi, Egyptian writer, psychiatrist and feminist, 'Exile and Resistance', Cairo, November 2002

How is it possible to have brothers and sisters and not be able to communicate with them? There were a thousand things I had to tell, to exchange ... I was alone, as only a tree knows how to be alone.

Ken Bugul, Senegalese writer, *The Abandoned Baobab*, 1984 (English translation 1991, p138)

When I was young I lay in the forest while the Cossacks murdered my family, and I cried out to the black empty sky: 'If there is a God let him strike me dead!' So I knew there was no God and I put my trust in men. When they failed me I cried: 'Eili, Eili, lama azavtani?' I was reproaching the God I didn't believe in for forsaking me. How can one live without faith in God, without faith in men? I am utterly, utterly alone.

Rose Zwi, South African novelist, *Another Year in Africa*, 1980, pp137-138

Ancestry

Angola,
you will not be the land of my
    birth
but you are the land of my womb.

Amélia Veiga, Portuguese-born Angolan poet, 'Angola', translated from the Portuguese by Julia Kirst (Chipasula & Chipasula, p155)

Weep not sister, you are not alone,
for you are just one branch of the tree –
The Tree of Life; The Tree of Africa

Ifi Amadiume, Nigerian poet, 'Nok Lady in Terracotta' (Chipasula & Chipasula, p71)

If you want to understand me
come, bend over this soul of Africa

Noémia de Sousa, Mozambican poet, 'If You Want to Know Me', *When Bullets Begin to Flower*, 1972, translated by Margaret Dickinson (Busby, p329)

Apartheid

Mention the 'Home to All' campaign and you will be
met either with a blank stare or the standard retorts,

'I didn't do anything,' 'I never supported apartheid,' 'I never treated my maid badly,' and the one that has survived the Holocaust: 'I didn't know' ... If you cannot see what apartheid did to your fellow South Africans, you must either be dead or living in Canada.

South African writer and journalist **Marianne Thamm**, 'Dead or living in Canada', 9 May 2001 (*Mental Floss*, 2002, p18)

The end of apartheid isn't the end of life, it's the beginning of everything else.

Nadine Gordimer, South African writer (Crwys-Williams, p23)

The task of reconstruction that is now with us is perhaps even more daunting than the fight for political emancipation.

Winnie Madikizela-Mandela, South African politician and former wife of Nelson Mandela, speaking at the American University in Washington DC, *The Citizen* (South Africa), 17 April 1996, p12

what will become of the rotten nation

Ingrid Jonker, South African poet, 'I Drift in the Wind', translated from Afrikaans by Jack Cope (Chipasula & Chipasula, p193)

And in the distance we can hear sounds of steadily running feet, steadfast feet, steady feet. And we know that these sounds that we hear are the sounds of those who are going to eradicate all this ugliness. These sounds that we hear are drawing nearer and nearer.

Dulcie September, South African writer and political activist, 'A Split Society – Fast Sounds on the Horizon', *One Never*

Knows: An Anthology of Black South African Women Writers,
1989 (Busby, p868)

The segregation, the setting of one off against
another – this breeds a corruption from which none
of us, whatever our colour, can be free.

Emma Mashinini, South African trade unionist, *Strikes Have
Followed Me All My Life*, 1989, p118

Life is not what it should be. After marriage you
do *not* live happily ever after. You shudder at the
thought of bringing into this world children to be in
the same unnatural plight as yourself, your parents
and your grandparents before you – passing on a
heritage of serfdom from one generation to another.
You are not human. Everything is a mockery.

Miriam Tlali, South African writer, *Muriel at Metropolitan*,
1975, p126

I was born on the sixth of July, 1937, in the
Pietermaritzburg Mental Hospital. The reason for my
peculiar birthplace was that my mother was white,
and she had acquired me from a black man. She
was judged insane, and committed to the mental
hospital while pregnant. Her name was Bessie
Emery and I consider it the only honour South
African officials ever did me – naming me after this
unknown, lovely, and unpredictable woman.

Bessie Head, South African-born Botswanan writer, *The Best
of South African Short Stories*, 1991, p324

Art

I came to realise that things aren't the most important in life. Instead, making things becomes the most important.

Maganthrie Pillay, South African filmmaker, 'Creating, Above All Else', by Nils van der Linden, 13 January 2005 (iafrica.com)

The arts are a valuable industry in any society.

Lola Shoneyin, Nigerian poet, interview with Nnorom Azuonye, 'My E-conversation with Lola Shoneyin', *Sentinel Poetry*, online magazine, February 2004

As an artist across the spectra of colour, race, gender and creed, my purpose of art making is to deal with relevant issues affecting our society at present. I believe artists are in the forefront of liberating and healing ourselves, and the society we exist within. Through art, we need to make our past, present and future work because as artists we have transcended the ordinary and live in highest form of imagination.

Payne Phalane, South African artist, quoted in 'Young, Black, and Gifted Womyn', by Z Muholi, *Behind the Mask* website, 26 January 2004

Thought-provoking creativity, what we know as ART, does not need a luxurious environment or a degree. Rather, it takes talent, and the willingness to notice the world around you, and it is born by connecting with people, environments, and who we are.

Zanele Muholi, South African artist, 'Young, Black, and Gifted Womyn', *Behind the Mask* website, 26 January 2004

The use of drama and the creative arts has been essential to all struggles all over the planet.

Lebogang Mashile, South African poet, biographies for the Centre for Creative Arts' International Festival of Poets, 26-31 May 2003

My dream is to spread African arts throughout the world; and to let the unborn generations know that our culture is very rich.

Nike Davies, Nigerian batik artist (nikeart.com)

... many objects that are meant to scare the living daylights out of you are shown with spotlights on them, totally putting the objects out of context. Such things make nonsense to a traditional African when he sees them... [it is like] wearing a bra on your bottom. That is not what it was designed for ... a mask doesn't come on its own. It comes with a costume. It comes with a festival ... It's man's contact with the gods.

Sokari Douglas Camp, Nigerian sculptress, *Africa Today*, March-April 1996, p42

Clay has such a fantastic personal feel. It's also therapeutic – when I'm tired and a bit tense, just by kneading and moulding the clay, I work out the tension through my hands.

Magdalene Odundo, Kenyan potter, 'Uncommon Clay', *Safari*, (magazine of the Inter-Continental Hotels Group), Vol. 9, No. 1, 1992, p21

Between the artist soul and God alone can ever
lie the awful answer to the question, Is my work
complete, is it the expression of truth as I know it?
   Olive Schreiner, South African writer, *Letters*, 1924
   (Buchanan-Gould, p103)

Authority

I can't stand empty Big Manism, something my
people do too well.
   Chimamanda Ngozi Adichie, Nigerian novelist, quoted in 'In
   the Footsteps of Chinua Achebe: Enter Chimamanda Ngozi
   Adichie, Nigeria's Newest Literary Voice', by Ike Anya, *Sentinel
   Poetry*, online magazine, November 2003

Authority derives from the way you conduct yourself, what you bring to the debate, rather than a
formal authority which only derives from your
position.
   Gill Marcus, South African politician, 1995 interview, *Cutting
   Through the Mountain*, p260

Beauty

There is beauty in simplicity.
   Chika Unigwe, Nigerian writer, interview with Nnorom
   Azuonye, 'My E-Conversation with Chika Unigwe', *Sentinel*,
   March 2003

Because the Arab/Berber men thought me to be
'pretty' they explained away their attraction by

reasoning that all Black African women who are
'pretty' are prostitutes.

> **Kola Boof**, Sudanese-American writer and activist, press
> statement, 3 January 2003 (www.kolaboof.com)

I have made history ... Black is beautiful.

> Words of Nigerian beauty queen **Agbani Darego**, the first black
> African to win the Miss World title, upon receiving her crown
> in 2001, in Sun City, South Africa (Bideh Williams, Newswatch
> Vol. 34 No. 22, 3 December 2001; Nigeriaworld.com)

So it was good to see the healthy young missionaries
and discover that some Whites were as beautiful as
we were ... then I was able to love them.

> **Tsitsi Dangarembga**, Zimbabwean writer, *Nervous Conditions*,
> 1988, p104

Another path, which conveniently twists as if in
conformity with the often unsteady feet that stumble
along it, brings you to the Happy Bar, the tin-roofed
dwelling where Maria Ssentamu's sumptuous curves
shake in perpetual merriment as she serves warm
beer in thick, greasy glasses to the thirsty locals.
Maria must surely weigh over fourteen stones. Never-
theless, she is by far the most seductive woman in
the village, and she has a number of children to prove
it. It seems that a simple shake of her magnificent
hips is enough to bowl a man over. Few can with-
stand the onslaught. Members of the Mother's Union
spitefully whisper that this unfailing charm is all
something to do with what Maria puts in the drinks.

Barbara Kimenye, Ugandan writer, *The Village*, 1965
(Strathern, p331)

The beautiful woman finds her fullness of bloom
only when a past has written itself on her ...
   Olive Schreiner, South African writer, *The Story of an African
   Farm*, 1883 (Penguin, 1995, p240)

Bravery and Courage

Courage is the chariot that redeems us in sin.
   Kola Boof, Sudanese-American writer and activist, *Long
   Train to the Redeeming Sin: Stories About African Women*, 2004
   (authors.aalbc.com)

In the history of the world and humanity, it is
always men and women of courage who show the
way and others follow.
   Theresa Kufuor, first lady of Ghana, Conference of African
   First Ladies on HIV/AIDS, Geneva, 17-19 July 2002

We all want the same thing: a decent life, peace,
love. And courage is what I, and all of us, must have,
always.
   Miriam Makeba, South African singer and civil rights activist,
   Makeba, My Story, 1988, back jacket text

I am she who cuts across the game reserve
That no girl crosses.
I am the boldest of the bold,
outfacer of wizards.

Obstinate perseverer,
The nation swore at me
and ate their words.
She cold shoulders kings and
despises mere commoners.

First verse of a **Zulu of South Africa** women's praise song
(Mapanje, p19)

Capitalism

Africa may have many reasons to blame herself,
but the world is not innocent about her. I think
that there is need for new approach to business
and international trade which puts people before
commodities and before profits.

Wangari Maathai, Kenyan environmental and human rights
activist, 'Bottle-Necks of Development in Africa', paper
presented at the 4th UN World Women's Conference in
Beijing, China, August-September 1995

We have been having terrible times here. You people
in England don't know what the heel of a capitalist
is when it gets right flat on the neck of a people! We
have an awful struggle before us in this country. It's
no case of not being allowed to fish in somebody
else's ground! You won't be allowed soon to have a
soul of *our* own. Now we are busy killing the poor
Matabele.

Olive Schreiner, South African writer, in a letter to Mr Alfred
Mattison, 13 April 1896 (Beeton, p48)

Censorship

People are still suffering from the relics of those oppressive regimes. So much was written but not publishable. Now we can let rip, read and write all the poems we had to hide during those times.
Lola Shoneyin, Nigerian poet, interview with Nnorom Azuonye, 'My E-conversation with Lola Shoneyin', *Sentinel Poetry*, online magazine, February 2004

The writing scene in South Africa is quite extraordinary. A flood of raw material by a population which was silenced for so long, a really necessary outlet. Poetry, workshops, theatre, and short stories abound, but no novels.
Sheila Fugard, English-South African novelist and poet, 1991 (Bruner, *African Women's Writing*, p95)

Literature is one of the few areas left where black and white feel some identity of purpose; we all struggle under censorship.
Nadine Gordimer, South African writer (Petras, p34)

Change

Legislation creates a framework to say these are the parameters within which you can act, but in terms of attitudes, you don't change an attitude overnight. Attitudes change because there are campaigns.
Unity Dow, High Court Judge of Botswana, interview with

Ian Henschke of the Australian Broadcasting Corporation, 3 October 2004

It is important to nurture any new ideas and initiatives which can make a difference for Africa.

Wangari Maathai, Kenyan environmental and human rights activist (www.brainyquote.com)

I enjoy drastic changes in life as long as I survive them.

Nawal El Saadawi, Egyptian writer, psychiatrist and feminist, 'Another World is Necessary', Porto Alegre, 28 January 2003

The modernity of today is the tradition of tomorrow.

Werewere Liking, Cameroonian playwright, interview with Michelle Mielly, Ki-Yi Village, Abidjan, Côte d'Ivoire, 2 June 2002 (African Postcolonial Literature in the Postcolonial Web)

When you sit in one place your ideas stay in that place.

Nike Davies, Nigerian batik artist (nikeart.com)

Sometimes unpredictable things happen and events gain a momentum of their own.

Farida Karodia, South African-Canadian writer, *A Shattering of Silence*, 1993, p1

My life is but a ten rand note
that can be used only because
there may be change.

Zindziswa Mandela, South African poet, *black as i am*, 1978

It is preferable to change the world on the basis of love of mankind. But if that quality be too rare, then common sense seems to be the next best thing.
Bessie Head, South African-born Botswanan writer (McKnight, p45)

For to men of the new ideas and the new light the great men of old look very small.
Olive Schreiner, South African writer, *Undine*, 1928 (Emslie, p153)

Do not be too anxious to change your old customs, your simple modes of life, your deep faiths, till you know what you are exchanging them for ... the day may come when South Africa and the world may have need of that which you have to offer.
Olive Schreiner, South African writer, *Thoughts on South Africa*, 1923 (Buchanan-Gould, p135)

Character and Conduct

... the world needs a global ethic with values which give meaning to life experiences and, more than religious institutions and dogmas, sustain the non-material dimension of humanity. Mankind's universal values of love, compassion, solidarity, caring and tolerance should form the basis for this global ethic which should permeate culture, politics, trade, religion and philosophy.

Wangari Maathai, Kenyan environmental and human rights activist, 'Bottle-Necks of Development in Africa', paper presented at the 4th UN World Women's Conference in Beijing, China, August-September 1995

It is not the conscious changes made in their lives by men and women – a new job, a new town, a divorce – which really shape them, like the chapter headings in a biography, but a long slow mutation of emotion, hidden, all-penetrative ...
Nadine Gordimer, South African writer, *The Lying Days*, 1953 (Petras, p34)

Men say it is so hard to do the right. I have never found that. The moment one knows what is right, I do it; it is easy to do it; the difficulty is to find what *is* right! There are such absolutely conflicting ideals ...
Olive Schreiner, South African writer, *From Man to Man*, 1927 (Emslie, p703)

Children

Trees are better than children; they bear fruit in your own lifetime.
Diane Awerbuck, South African writer, *Gardening at Night*, 2003, p20

Every child needs at least two or three adults who are irrationally committed to that child ... a child is a social being who needs to be brought up by people. So when they grow up on the streets, or the parents are not there, it is really a crisis for the future of that country.

Inonge Mbikusita Lewanika, Zambian diplomat, interview with the International Youth Foundation, May 2003

One thing is certain: here in Kuito, children push the world onwards to infinity.

Ana Paula Taveres, Angolan poet, 'Kuito, A Child's Map of War and Infinity – Photographs and Poetry Regarding Angolan Conflict', *UNESCO Courier*, July 2001

Our precious jewels, the children, have borne the impact of the effects of the civil crisis. Exposure to war, potent drugs and other deviant behaviour, and the persistent closure of schools have all added more complex dimensions to the already poor conditions of our children ... as a mother, I consider the children and their future my highest priority.

Ruth Perry, first African woman president (Liberia), speaking during the Abuja First Ladies Summit, May 1997

A society that does not care about the well-being of its children is a society without a future. A society that 'devours' its children is on its way to destruction because it is breaking the life cycle.

Calixthe Beyala, Cameroonian novelist, *Your Name Shall Be Tanga* [*Tu t'appelleras Tanga*], 1988 (iupjournals.org)

Everything was costing her money, money she didn't have. Adim's schoolwork began to suffer and

the boy was losing weight. It was true what they
said, she thought, that if you don't have children
the longing for them will kill you, and if you do, the
worrying over them will ...

Buchi Emecheta, Nigerian writer, *The Joys of Motherhood*,
1979, p212

O my child, now indeed I am happy.
Now indeed I am a wife –
No more a bride, but a Mother-of-one.
Be splendid and magnificent, child of desire ...
Child, child, child, love I have had for my man.
But now, only now, have I the fullness of love.

Didinga (Sudan) song from a mother to her first-born (Busby,
p5)

Cinema

Film-making is a man's world at the moment, but
we have a right to be here.

Maganthrie Pillay, South African filmmaker, 'Creating, Above
All Else', by Nils van der Linden, 13 January 2005 (iafrica.com)

The stories tend to be quite simple but very
dramatic and heavy on the emotions: the women
wail and are avaricious money lovers; the men are
just as emotional and very vengeful. Throw in a
gibbering bone-rattling juju man and Bible-waving
preacher and what you have is a brew of conflict,

revenge, trials and tribulations ...

On films from Nollywood, Nigeria's movie industry, Zambian-based journalist **Helen Muchimba**, 'Nigerian Film Lights Zambia's Screens', *BBC Focus on Africa Magazine*, 23 September 2004

This modern art form could preserve something from Africa's culture and further our education, especially because literacy rates were not so high.

Mahen Bonetti, cinema curator from Sierra Leone, interview with Horst Rutsch, *The UN Chronicle Online Edition*

... It is magical to see Africans' reaction to cinema. People walk miles and miles to come and see movies in packed open-air stadiums. People jostle and push, even hang on trees to see these films. They really want to see images of themselves, to hear their voices, to see their own faces on the screen.

Mahen Bonetti, cinema curator from Sierra Leone, interview with Horst Rutsch, *The UN Chronicle Online Edition*

American films gave me hope. Hindu films gave me melodies.

Ramata Diakité, Malian singer (Afropop Worldwide website, contribution by Banning Eyre)

... it's really important to me that there is a cohesive voice. Too often we fragment ourselves. What are we as African people doing to reclaim honor? For me, [cinema] is a way to unify and consolidate all we have to improve tomorrow for our children.

Mahen Bonetti, cinema curator from Sierra Leone, 'Reclaiming Honor; African Film Fest Hopes to Challenge Perceptions', interview with Jacque Lynn Schiller, *indieWire. com*, 5 April 2002

Colonialism

In the revolutionary school
I know why I study –
But in the colonial school
I was studying like the blind …

Elisa de Silveira, Mozambican secondary school student, 1978 (Searle, title pages)

On his left, silhouetted against the sky, the turrets of Nauheim Castle stood fortress-like in their gaunt isolation – Nauheim – one of the many castles which still dot the sandy wastes of South West Africa, heartbreak castles his mother had called them, built by rich German settlers before the First World War – settlers who lived in a strange and grandiose isolation, with all the trappings and ceremony of the fatherland.

Elizabeth Jonsson, South African writer, 'The Silver Sky', *The Silver Sky and Other Stories*, c. 1974 (*The Best of South African Short Stories*, 1991, p261)

That was one of the things she held against the missionaries: how they stressed Christ's submission to humiliation, and so had conditioned the people of

Africa to humiliation by the white man.

Nadine Gordimer, South African writer, 'Not for Publication', *Not for Publication and Other Stories*, 1965 (Partnow, *The Quotable Woman*, p274)

The Europeans ... found a lot of tyranny and oppression here, people being beaten and killed and sold into slavery ... We Habe [i.e. Hausa] wanted them to come, it was the Fulani who did not like it. When the Europeans came the Habe saw that if you worked for them then they paid you for it. Then didn't say, like the Fulani, 'Commoner, give me this! Commoner, bring me that!' Yes, the Habe wanted them, they saw no harm in them.

Baba, an old Hausa woman of Nigeria, quoted in M F Smith's *Baba of Karo*, London, 1964, pp67-68 (Hallett, p300)

Tell that all the community is to rise again from the dead! Tell that all cattle must be slaughtered, for they are herded by hands defiled with witchcraft!

Nongqause, Xhosa prophet, who believed that witchcraft was responsible for the encroachment of foreigners on her people's land; following the slaughter of their cattle 20 000 Xhosa starved to death (www.whoosh.org/issue35)

Communism

Perhaps it is that the result of having been a communist is to be a humanist.

Doris Lessing, English-Zimbabwean author (Bloom, p54)

What hypocrites, I said inside me, to say communists had misled me into wanting to change the
system. I didn't need any communists to tell me
apartheid is evil.

Joyce Sikakane, South African writer, *A Window on Soweto*,
1977 (Busby, p560)

Complacency and Denial

I speak for myself alone and I am interested in
presenting things as they are and in challenging our
collective hypocrisy. I remember being blasted by
an Igbo web group, about two years ago, because
of a story about a teenager who had a boyfriend.
A boyfriend! We prefer sometimes to cover our
heads with our hands and pretend that things do
not happen. Until we acknowledge things to be the
way they are, we cannot own them, and we cannot
control them.

Chimamanda Ngozi Adichie, Nigerian novelist, quoted in 'In
the Footsteps of Chinua Achebe: Enter Chimamanda Ngozi
Adichie, Nigeria's Newest Literary Voice', by Ike Anya, *Sentinel
Poetry*, online magazine, November 2003

The chains … represent our desire for control,
certainty, ease and honor. It is our fear of losing our
chains that keeps us where we are.

Words of a female sangoma, speaking in South African **Ruth
Tearle**'s organisational transformation book *Ride the Wild
Tiger*, 2000, p222

There were no newspapers to be seen around her house, that house where she thought herself safe among trees, safe from the threat of him and his kind, safe from the present.

Nadine Gordimer, South African writer, 'Safe Houses', *Jump and Other Stories*, 1991, p209

Complicity and Fault

The genocide cannot be characterized as a humanitarian drama. This would mean refusing to analyse the way a genocide is able to be carried out ... Generalizations favor the killers: I was saved by a Hutu.

Yolande Mukagasana, Rwandan nurse and human rights advocate, interview with Nicoletta Fagiolo, UNHCR, October 2000

The house of the local 'Mayor' was also burnt down ... I remembered what he had said a few weeks back in a Residents' meeting.

'You seem to forget that I am as black as you are, and I suffer just like you do under the apartheid laws of this country.' The grumbling from the audience showed that nobody believed him.

Gcina Mhlope, South African actress and writer, 'It's Quiet Now' (*The Best of South African Short Stories*, 1991, p453)

I have seen enough to know that blame does not come in neatly packaged parcels.

Tsitsi Dangarembga, Zimbabwean writer, *Nervous Conditions*, 1988 (2001 edition, p12)

The greatest devil among us has his white spots, and the purest saint has ink-black stains which will be clearly visible if he do[es] not keep his white clothing too tight about him.

Olive Schreiner, South African writer, *Undine*, 1928 (Emslie, p82)

Conflict

We are sharing our resources in a very inequitable way. We have parts of the world that are very deprived and parts of the world that are very rich. And that is partly the reason why we have conflicts.

Wangari Maathai, Kenyan environmental and human rights activist (quoted in the Nobel Peace Prize presentation speech delivered by Professor Ole Danbolt Mjøs, 10 December 2004)

For as long as one is human, one is destined to deal with conflict. A good dose of humour and some willingness to take risks give one the chance not only to transcend artificial boundaries but to derive deep pleasure in doing so.

Mamphela Ramphele, South African doctor and academic (*Great South Africans*, 2004, p162)

Contentment

Don't talk to me of change, even of freedom:
I have seen changes and I am content
> **Marjorie Oludhe Macgoye**, English-born Kenyan poet, 'For Miriam' (Chipasula & Chipasula, p120)

'Bala Bala' means 'the essence of things' in Fon. The lines on our hands – can we change them? No. We are born with them, and that's the way it is. There are certain things in this lifetime of ours that we just have to accept, and we shouldn't be judgmental.
> **Angélique Kidjo**, Beninois musician (www.giantstep.net)

There are times in life when everything seems dark, when the brain reels and we cannot see that there is anything but death, but, if we wait long enough, after long, long years, calm comes. It may be we cannot say it was well; but we are contented, we accept the past. The struggle has ended.
> **Olive Schreiner**, South African writer (Buchanan-Gould, p 91)

Corruption

Madagascar is one of the poorest countries in the world, brought to its knees by corrupt politicians and businessmen.
> **Hanitra Rasoanaivo**, London-based singer with the Malagasy band Tarika ('African War and Peace', by Nigel Williamson, *Times* newspapers, 1997)

Corruption is a serious cancer in Africa and it is eating into every aspect of life and into every socio-economic group. The misery it brings to ordinary Africans and the opportunity it provides to non-Africans to exploit Africa is reminiscent of the exploits of the Slave Trade. Today's African leaders are comparable to the African slave barons who facilitated the capturing and the selling-off of millions of their fellow blacks to distant lands where they were subjugated into slavery, only today they are subdued within their own borders.

Wangari Maathai, Kenyan environmental and human rights activist, 'Bottle-Necks of Development in Africa', paper presented at the 4th UN World Women's Conference in Beijing, China, August-September 1995

Why is this type of a crime tolerated by the international community? … Perhaps it is time there were economic crimes against humanity.

Wangari Maathai, Kenyan environmental and human rights activist, 'Bottle-Necks of Development in Africa', paper presented at the 4th UN World Women's Conference in Beijing, China, August-September 1995

The greatest nations, like the greatest individuals, have often been the poorest; and with wealth comes often what is more terrible than poverty – corruption.

Olive Schreiner, South African writer, *An English South African's View of the Situation*, *c.* 1899 (Partnow, *The New Quotable Woman*, p224)

Crime

Pa Visagie, like most people, had adopted the fear.
The new government was soft on crime. Young
offenders were set free. Rapists got bail. The death
penalty had been scrapped. If you reported someone
to the police, you feared revenge.

Rayda Jacobs, South African author, 'Postcards from South
Africa', *Post-Cards from South Africa*, 2004, p173

I could go on contemplating the deep lines of alien-
ation that scar Jo'burg society until I'm blue in the
face. But I'd still have to scream: Hey, man, it's not
OK.

Heidi Holland, South African journalist and writer, 'Getting
Even', *From Jo'burg to Jozi*, 2002, p110

… because there isn't enough money for everyone,
millions live by stealing and plundering and murder-
ing and lying and all sorts of things to get hold of
money – and the rest pretend they're alive, while
they're living behind stronger and stronger bars.

Dalene Matthee, South African novelist, *The Day the Swallows
Spoke*, 1992, p173

God's own country for a get-away.

Character speaking on South Africa in the 1920s short story
'Blind Justice', by South African writer **Ethelreda Lewis**
(Dodd, p91)

Criticism

I generally don't stick labels on myself but I don't
have any problems with others doing so, partly
because critics are not happy unless they've done so
… Readers and critics will develop their views based
on their perspective. You see a man lying by the side
of the road, he's either sleeping, drunk, taking an
afternoon nap or maybe even dead. It all depends on
how close you look and what angle you are looking
from.

Lola Shoneyin, Nigerian poet, interview with Nnorom
Azuonye, 'My E-conversation with Lola Shoneyin', *Sentinel
Poetry*, online magazine, February 2004

The critics slap labels on you and then expect you to
talk inside their terms.

Doris Lessing, English-Zimbabwean author, 'Doris Lessing
on Feminism, Communism, and "Space Fiction" ', by Lesley
Hazelton, *The New York Times*, 25 July 1982

Culture

Culture plays a central role in the political, economic
and social life of communities. Indeed, culture may
be the missing link in the development of Africa.
Culture is dynamic and evolves over time, con-
sciously discarding retrogressive traditions, like
female genital mutilation (FGM), and embracing

aspects that are good and useful. Africans, especially, should re-discover positive aspects of their culture.

Wangari Maathai, Kenyan environmental and political activist, Nobel Lecture after receiving the Nobel Peace Prize, Oslo, Norway, 10 December 2004

I don't want to disappear.

On the disintegration of Senegalese culture, **Sokhna Benga**, Senegalese scriptwriter and novelist, 'Transformation: An Informal Journal about Yari Yari Pamberi 2004', by Felicia Pride, November 2004 (www.thebacklist.net)

Everybody needs a backbone. If we do not refer to the old traditions, it is almost like operating with amnesia.

Ama Ata Aidoo, Ghanaian writer (www.kirjasto.sci.fi/aidoo.htm)

'Cultural values.' That term worries me, especially when it is used next to Africa because I have found that we sometimes use it to shield our hypocrisies and to perpetuate the lies we tell ourselves. I love the culture of my people, but at the same time, I do not believe in idealizing, or in transporting it to its 'pure' past.

Chimamanda Ngozi Adichie, Nigerian novelist, 'In the Footsteps of Chinua Achebe: Enter Chimamanda Ngozi Adichie, Nigeria's Newest Literary Voice', by Ike Anya, *Sentinel Poetry*, online magazine, November 2003

They can take our diamonds away from us and every other material resource, but not our culture. We have to hold on to something. Man does not survive without culture.

Mahen Bonetti, Sierra-Leonean organiser of the New York African Film Festival (Rob Wright, 'Africa's Film Capital', *Africa Report*, 1 January 1995)

To identify with the country of your adoption is not necessarily to lose your culture.

Fatima Meer, South African liberation struggle leader and writer (*Great South Africans*, 2004, p142)

Dance

There are few social levellers as effective as standing in line with 80 other people for a formation version of the Achy Breaky dance.

Pnina Fenster, South African magazine editor (Crwys-Williams, p108)

They played the new rumba that, as popular music will, pointed unsystematic fingers at the conditions of the times: 'I'll beat you up if you keep asking for your money', 'Father, I am jobless, give me money for roora', 'My love, why have you taken a second wife?' There was swaying of hips, stamping of feet to the pulse of these social facts.

Tsitsi Dangarembga, Zimbabwean writer, *Nervous Conditions*, 1988 (2001 edition, p4)

All the dancing I've done has been alone in the veld, when I've jumped in the air and thrown up my arms and shouted with the mere joy of living.

Olive Schreiner, South African writer (Crwys-Williams, p108)

Daughters

What I hope for her is that she has that love for the world and those things that you can't buy.

Sade, Nigerian singer, speaking about her daughter, interview with Lonnae O'Neal Parker, *Essence*, March 2001

Our own parents have a lot to answer for committing us to misery. They destroy us the moment they choose to send boys to school, leaving us girls at home. Their thinking is that we will get married and thereafter live happily forever. This is crooked thinking as there is nothing like that. Not sending daughters to school is the same as raising slaves.

Women in Zimbabwe, quoted in Getecha and Chipika, *Zimbabwe Women's Voices*, 1995, pp24, 33 (The African Woman Food Farmer Initiative; www.thp.org)

Father, let me go to school too
Even though I am a girl
You never know where fortune lies

First lines of 'A Girl is a Child Too', by Zimbabwean poet **Shumirai Makasa**, Getecha and Chipika, *Zimbabwe Women's Voices*, 1995, p35 (The African Woman Food Farmer Initiative; www.thp.org)

In the rural areas, when you don't have daughters, life is very hard – in fact, it's slavery.

Issa Hadiza, farmer from Niger, 'Women's Work: Africa's Precious Resource', The Hunger Project, September 1992, pp17, 21 (The African Woman Food Farmer Initiative; www.thp.org)

Sing daughter sing
around you are
uncountable tunes

From the poem 'Where are those Songs?' by Kenyan poet **Micere Githae Mugo** (The African Woman Food Farmer Initiative; www.thp.org)

Yes they want sons, but they always say that to beget a daughter first is a blessing to the family. A daughter caters for the well-being of her parents in their old age, sons only care for their immediate families. They care little for their ageing parents. A son caters for continuity of the family-name and external image, but a daughter caters for love, understanding and unity within the family circle … Our people believe that it is a curse to beget only sons and no daughter. They will not put up with a chieftain who has no daughter. They say that his homestead is standing on spikes and sooner or later will be razed to the dust.

Catherine Obianuju Acholonu, Nigerian writer and poet, 'Mother was a Great Man' (Bruner, *African Women's Writing*, p11)

But how was she to tell this beautiful creature that … though a girl may be counted as one child, to her people a boy was like four children put together?

41

And if the family could give the boy a good university education, his mother would be given the status of a man in the tribe. How was she to explain all that?

Buchi Emecheta, Nigerian writer, *Second-Class Citizen*, 1974, chapter 6 (Partnow, *The New Quotable Woman*, p500)

Death

The land is gathering into its depths the people who pass over her surface.

Alexandra Fuller, British journalist and writer who grew up in Zimbabwe, *Don't Let's Go to the Dogs Tonight*, 2002

Fighters never say goodbye.

Graça Machel, Mozambican educator and politician, written in a letter to Winnie Madikizela-Mandela after her husband, Samora Moisés Machel, first president of Mozambique, died in a plane crash in 1986 (Christie)

Death, the tenuous passage between two opposite worlds, one tumultuous, the other still.

Mariama Bâ, Senegalese writer, *So Long a Letter*, 1979 (1981 edition, p2)

Eternal death has worked like a warrior rat, with diabolical sense of duty, to gnaw my bottom. Everything is finished now.

Ama Ata Aidoo, Ghanaian writer, 'The Message', *No Sweetness Here*, 1970 (1995 edition, p43)

Death knocks at your door, and before you can tell him to come in, he is in the house with you.

Grace Ogot, Kenyan writer (Petras, p62)

It was unbelievably beautiful, the shape of death ...

Doris Lessing, English-Zimbabwean author, *The Golden Notebook*, 1962 (Bloom, p44)

Madonna! Madonna!

Last words of the Sudanese Catholic saint **Josephine Bakhita** when she died on 8 February 1947 in Schio, Italy

... that subtle charm that death alone gives to men or times ...

Olive Schreiner, South African writer, *Undine*, 1928 (Emslie, p49)

The thing which you call death is the father of all life and beauty. Till life goes, till blood flows, no higher life can come.

Olive Schreiner, South African writer, *Undine*, 1928 (Emslie, p176)

Decay and Decline

The country is in ruins. Nothing works any more. There are no schools, no hospitals, nothing ... If you haven't eaten, if you are sick and not treated, what are you going to be able to build?

Esther Kamatari, Burundian princess and former fashion model, interview with Associated Press Television News regarding her presidential candidacy, 'Burundian Princess for President' by Tori Foxcroft, 24 December 2004 (www.news.24. com)

Once prosperous, once the pearl of Africa,
Once the pride of its people,
Now sundered by hatred, soured by grief . . .
Assumpta Acam-Oturu, Ugandan poet, 'An Agony . . . A Resurrection' (Chipasula & Chipasula, p143)

Society had created barriers so that relationships would fail and that all that was human would decay. The human marvel.
Ken Bugul, Senegalese writer, *The Abandoned Baobab*, 1984 (English translation 1991, p153)

Why, when a nation or a race or a dominant class has reached a certain point of culture and material advance, has it always seemed to fall back from it, and the nation or race or class to be swept away?
Olive Schreiner, South African writer, *From Man to Man*, 1927 (Emslie, p510)

Deceit and Lying

and all the words falling from his mouth
have become lies
Kola Boof, Sudanese-American writer and activist, from her poem 'The Blind Eye of Forever' (poetwomen.50megs.com)

Lies never give you joy and peace.
Angélique Kidjo, Beninois musician (www.giantstep.net)

Innocence as good manners is nothing but deceit.
Calixthe Beyala, Cameroonian author, *Naked Woman Black Woman* [*Femme nue Femme noire*], 2003 (translation by Sybille N Nyeck) (thewitness.org)

The splendid emotions of a love affair are the luxurious furnishings of the lie.
Nadine Gordimer, South African writer, 'A Journey', *Jump and Other Stories*, 1991, p157

It would not take more faith and prayer to obtain pardon for one lie than for twenty; and Cousin Jonathan, having told one, found that lies flow as easily as truths if only one is used to them.
Olive Schreiner, South African writer, *Undine*, 1928 (Emslie, p81)

Defiance

You have left us with no friends, so I have to accept awards from our enemies.
Helen Suzman, South African parliamentarian, in reply to President PW Botha when he condemned her for going to the USA to receive an award from one of South Africa's enemies (*Great South Africans*, 2004, p100)

I didn't keep quiet under apartheid, and I won't be silent now.
South African journalist **Charlene Smith** (www.safrica.info)

... word got round that Katie Fortuin had gone to sleep because of Group Areas, in resistance to it. Then, because people always talk and dream and imagine, it was circulated that Katie wasn't going to wake up till justice returned. Our cottage became something of a shrine to a woman who turned herself into a barometer of oppression, who refused to be moved.

Finuala Dowling, South African writer and poet, 'The Awakening of Katie Fortuin', 1996 (Medalie, p184)

You have tampered with woman, you have struck a rock.

South African Women's Protest Slogan (McKnight, p49)

I've learned in my early childhood that women's will can make any law encroaching upon her null and void.

Dorreya Shafik, Egyptian women's rights activist (www. iearneqgypt.org)

The child is not dead
the child lifts his fists against his mother
who shouts Afrika! shouts the breath
of freedom and the veld ...

Ingrid Jonker, South African poet, first lines of 'The Child who was Shot Dead by Soldiers at Nyanga', 1961 (Gray, *Southern African Verse*, p250)

'Tell Mr. Rhodes,' she said, 'that his nose is also only a small point. Let him cut it off and then look into the mirror.'

Marie Koopmans de Wet, South African socialite and preservationist, in reply to a request by Cecil John Rhodes that she agree to have one of the five points of the Old Castle of Good Hope in Cape Town cut off to make way for an electric tramway (as recorded by Elsa Smithers, *March Hare*, p148)

I will sneer at ridiculous rules and people ...

Aisha al-Taimuriya, 19th century Egyptian poet, *Hilyat al-Tiraz (Embroidered Ornaments)* (Petras, p97)

Democracy

Responsible governance of the environment was impossible without democratic space. Therefore, the tree became a symbol for the democratic struggle in Kenya.

Wangari Maathai, Kenyan environmental and political activist, Nobel Lecture after receiving the Nobel Peace Prize, Oslo, Norway, 10 December 2004

When I unfolded the ballot, the full national choice lay under my hand. For the first time. It was as if a miracle burst open like a small seed-casing in my throat. For the first time I am part of my complete country.

Antjie Krog, South African poet and writer, *A Change of Tongue*, 2003, p31

You need the freedom of association. You need the freedom of information. You need the freedom to challenge and to monitor government and other officials. Without that kind of society, democracy becomes a ritual.

Frene Ginwala, Speaker of South Africa's Parliament, speaking at the Global Coalition for Africa, 27-28 November 1996 (*Africa Recovery*, United Nations, May 1996, p25)

A democracy for me is not simply about majority rule. It is also about the right of the person who disagrees to disagree, within the parameters of non-violence.

Gill Marcus, South African politician, 1995 interview, *Cutting Through the Mountain*, p262

Dependency

Women are capable of living for so many other reasons than men.

Buchi Emecheta, Nigerian writer, interviewed by Julie Holmes in *The Voice*, 9 July 1996

I have often asked myself why I didn't get up and go. Is it perhaps the spirit of those old ancestresses of mine who for millions of years have followed the man over steppes and through deserts and across mountains, with stripes and burdens, always following, following, following, – which today cries out in us, 'Follow – follow – till he sets you free!'

Olive Schreiner, South African writer, *From Man to Man*, 1927 (Emslie, p574)

Determination

You have to have goals; you have to have dreams. You have to work at what you believe in and you have to believe in yourself.

Natalie du Toit, South African Paralympic gold medallist in swimming (*Great South Africans*, 2004, p148)

I think when the world record belongs to someone else, then you have to break it.

Penny Heyns, South African breaststroke swimmer (*Great South Africans*, 2004, p156)

Diamonds

A diamond is just a piece of charcoal with a finer education.

Dalene Matthee, South African novelist, *The Day the Swallows Spoke*, 1992, p11

These most brilliant of precious stones were a severe temptation to many otherwise honest people.

Elsa Smithers, South African farmer, *March Hare*, 1935, p137

She was attracted, like all others who were near enough to feel its influence, by the great magnet that draws to itself all who are good-for-nothing vagabonds, wanderers, or homeless – the Diamond Fields.

Olive Schreiner, South African writer, *Undine*, 1928 (Emslie, p117)

You have got to be joking. I will never take your hard-earned money for a worthless pebble. Take it. The children, I am sure, will pick up many more.

Mrs Jacobs speaking in March 1867 to Schalk van Niekerk who wanted to buy a shiny pebble that her children were playing with in Hopetown, south of what is now Kimberley, South Africa; the pebble turned out to be the 'Eureka' 10-carat diamond, the first diamond found in South Africa (De Villiers, p123)

Dictatorship

Dictatorship … characterizes all ruling systems whether in the East or the West. The degree of dictatorship may vary from country to country. Throughout history but more so in our days, a small minority decides and dictates behind a veneer of democracy. In some countries of the European or American continents people enjoy some personal freedom labelled 'democracy', but nowhere do people decide what will happen to them in their political, economic or cultural life, public or private.

Nawal El Saadawi, Egyptian writer, psychiatrist and feminist, 'Towards a Philosophy that will Awaken the Conscience of the Human Race', paper presented at the Sixth International Conference of the Arab Women's Solidarity Association, Cairo, 3-5 January 2002

Look,
Oh heartless dictators,
people are dying, dying,

dying of hunger,
dying of thirst!

> Last stanza of the poem 'We Have Even Lost Our Tongues!' by
> Nigerian poet **Ifi Amadiume** (Chipasula & Chipasula, p86)

Dignity

My whole nation is graceful. Nobody has to tell us
how to walk or how to stand. We have an air, a
dignity: Whatever happens you keep your head up.

> **Iman**, Somali supermodel (Copage, p December 7)

If I have any advice worth giving to the rising generation of Africa, it is this: NEVER be ashamed of your
colour. Be representative of the best of African life.
I found from experience that this is the only way to
happiness, the only way to retain one's self-respect,
the only way to win the respect of other races,
and the only way in which we can ever give a real
contribution to the world.

> **Adelaide Casely-Hayford**, writer and educator from Sierra
> Leone (Busby, p154)

Disappointment and Disillusionment

I did not ask for anything, not for a pension nor
even for a needle. We worked for the sake of God
and for our beliefs. But now, to tell the truth, I regret
it, I regret my daughters.

Fatma Bedj, Algerian woman who lost three children in the fight for independence, quoted in an article in *The Middle East* magazine, Chris Kutschera, April 1996 (www.Chris-Kutschera.com)

The independence? Nothing of what I had hoped for was achieved. I had expected that my children would be able to have an education but they did not get it. We were poor peasants then, we are poor peasants now. Nothing has changed. Everything is the same. The only thing is that we are free, the war is over, we work without fear – but apart from that, nothing has changed.

Halima Ghomri, woman fighter in the Algerian war of independence against France, quoted in an article in *The Middle East* magazine, Chris Kutschera, April 1996 (www.Chris-Kutschera.com)

Oh, she ought to have known, at her age ought not to expect the unattainable ever to be anything other than itself.

Zoë Wicomb, South African writer, 'A Trip to the Gifberge', 1987 (Medalie, p131)

Throughout my life I've had to support parties, causes, nations, and movements which stink.

Doris Lessing, English-Zimbabwean author, interview at Stony Brook, New York, May 1969 (Bloom, p78)

Divorce

Leave one man, marry another. What is the difference?

Character speaking in Ghanaian writer **Ama Ata Aidoo**'s novel *Changes: A Love Story*, 1991

People marry younger, to divorce earlier to remarry their 'lost' youth.

Nina van Vliet, South African chemist, 'Oh, But is the Woman of a Lifetime' (Van der Laan, p101)

After all, what was a wedding, he had asked. You are simply being licensed. If you feel the necessity, you become licensed, then you become unlicensed, and if you have either youth or energy, you become licensed again. Why make a fuss?

Sheila Roberts, South African writer, 'The Wedding', 1973 (*The Best of South African Short Stories*, 1991, p358)

She married him, briefly but – as she said when it was all over – for long enough.

Doris Lessing, English-Zimbabwean author, 'Side Benefits of an Honourable Profession', *The Story of a Non-Marrying Man and Other Stories*, 1972 (1990 edition, p86)

Doctors and Medicine

Green vegetables and fresh fruit – they are too poor for the luxury of these remedies, what they have come to the clinic for is a bottle of medicine.

Nadine Gordimer, South African writer, *The House Gun*, 1998 (1999 paperback, p14)

While patients expect their doctors to be technically conversant, they also require a little soul.
Hedi Lampert-Kemper, South African journalist (Crwys-Williams, p121)

Of the hospital he had this to say, 'How can a stranger know the diseases of the people? What does he know about the wrath of the gods of my ancestors? Let those that are beginning to go funny in the head swallow white clay for medicine and have their stomachs slit open for a cure.'
Zaynab Alkali, Nigerian novelist, *The Stillborn*, 1984 (Busby, p789)

... the kaffir turns to the witch doctor to enlist the powers of darkness on his side. He is a firm believer in the efficacy of charms and potions and in the sacrifice of animals and birds. Lion fat is one of the most potent charms and is greatly prized.
Elsa Smithers, South African farmer, *March Hare*, 1935, p155

Dreams and Escapism

Timbuktu was (and still is) a dream-feeder.
Antjie Krog, South African poet and writer, *A Change of Tongue*, 2003, p287

Your goals are your dreams and your dreams alone.
If you do not bring your goals out of your dreams
and into reality, no one would.

Dorothy A Atabong, Cameroonian actress and writer (www.
roadtoromance.ca)

Southern Africa might one day become the home of
the storyteller and dreamer, who did not hurt others
but only introduced new dreams that filled the heart
with wonder.

Bessie Head, South African-born Botswanan writer, *The Best
of South African Short Stories*, 1991, p326

One could dream one's life, but one couldn't dream
one's reality. The everyday is made up of nothing
but isolated moments.

Ken Bugul, Senegalese writer, *The Abandoned Baobab*, 1984
(English translation 1991, p14)

Education

How can I have a voice when there is no school?

Lina Magaia, Mozambican writer, 'Transformation: An
Informal Journal about Yari Yari Pamberi 2004', by Felicia
Pride, November 2004 (www.thebacklist.net)

The privilege of a higher education, especially outside Africa, broadened my original horizon and
encouraged me to focus on the environment, women
and development in order to improve the quality of

life of people in my country in particular and in the African region in general.

Wangari Maathai, Kenyan environmental and human rights activist (www.brainyquote.com)

His grandfather had looked at him for a long time and then he'd said calmly, I thought you wanted to become a warrior. And he'd replied proudly, yes, grandfather, I *am* becoming a warrior, but you taught me that it is not necessary for a warrior to hold a spear in his hand for all to see; when the time comes I'll bring out the gun and fight the enemy and chase him away and then with my school certificate I'll get a good job and bring wealth to all our people.

Violet Dias Lannoy, Mozambican writer, 'The Story of Jesus …' (Bruner, *African Women's Writing*, p64)

Egypt and North Africa

It is tempting to declare that all Africans should at some time embark on a pilgrimage to Egypt – if only to collide with the realization that this continent was once, indeed, the very centre of the world.

Shannon Sherry, South African journalist, 'River of Time', *Mail&Guardian* (South Africa), 23-29 May 2003, pII

Sudan is a Taliban-like terrorist nation where the Bashir regime can DECREE anything they bloody well like.

Kola Boof, Sudanese-American writer and activist, press statement, 3 January 2003 (www.kolaboof.com)

In the desert there is no need for pretence ...
Nothing matters except the eternal.
> **Malika Oufkir**, Moroccan heiress imprisoned with her family for twenty years, and Michèle Fitoussi, *Stolen Lives, Twenty Years in a Desert Jail*, 1999, p288

My country is an asylum where madmen
Speak with their eyes
> First lines of the poem 'The Dead Erect' by Algerian poet **Malika O'Lahsen**, translated from the French by Eric Sellin (Chipasula & Chipasula, p9)

Egyptians are the most welcoming and friendly people in the world. Our ancient temples and wonders are the most beautiful. The sun shines on the Nile. 'Welcome to Egypt,' the people in the streets cry out to strangers. 'Welcome in our home.' Anyone considering a vacation to Egypt should not postpone it.
> **Jehan Sadat**, wife of Egyptian president Anwar Sadat, *A Woman of Egypt*, 1987, p464

Environmentalism

Today we are faced with a challenge that calls for a shift in our thinking, so that humanity stops threat-ening its life-support system. We are called to assist

the Earth to heal her wounds and in the process
to heal our own – indeed, to embrace the whole
creation in all its diversity, beauty and wonder.

Wangari Maathai, Kenyan environmental and human rights
activist, Nobel Lecture after receiving the Nobel Peace Prize,
Oslo, Norway, 10 December 2004

We have a special responsibility to the ecosystem
of this planet. In making sure that other species
survive we will be ensuring the survival of our own.

Wangari Maathi, Kenyan environmental and human rights
activist, 1980s (www:The Right Livelihood Award, 1984)

Were a large tract of this country granted or bought
at a nominal price, and freedom from intrusion
guaranteed, and were the interests of scientific
Europe and America aroused and directed to this
matter, and a body of scientific men and practical
travellers formed for the direction and management
of the scheme, it might pass into the region of the
practical and obtainable … In Central and Southern
African to-day primitive nature is making its last
stand on the surface of the globe.

On creating wildlife reserves, **Olive Schreiner**, South African
writer, *Thoughts on South Africa*, 1923 (1992 edition, pp322, 324)

Equality between the sexes

The world cannot go forward unless men and
women work in partnership to make it a better place.

Unity Dow, High Court Judge of Botswana, interview with Ian Henschke of the Australian Broadcasting Corporation, 3 October 2004

I believe that both the male and the female are co-dependent on each other. Neither of the two should exist exclusively. That is obvious in my works. I must add though that I am [a] firm believer in the re-structuring of power so that women in many societies get a fair share of it.

Chika Unigwe, Nigerian writer, interview with Nnorom Azuonye, 'My E-Conversation with Chika Unigwe', *Sentinel*, March 2003

The only ritual in which we are afforded the same status as men is at our funeral. It is in death that we ultimately achieve equality. Almost every other little parade, charade or ceremony serves either overtly or, cowering under the cloak of ancient wisdom and truth, to reinforce our role as perpetual, shuffling servants to patriarchy.

South African writer and journalist **Marianne Thamm**, 'A snip away', 11 September 2002 (*Mental Floss*, 2002, p112)

Always in our dreams we hear the turn of the key that shall close the last brothel; the clink of the last coin that pays for the body and soul of a woman; the falling of the last wall that encloses artificially the activity of woman and divides her from man; always we picture the love of the sexes, as, once a dull, slow creeping worm; then a torpid earthly chrysalis; at

last the fine winged insect, glorious in the sunshine
of the future.

Olive Schreiner, South African writer, *Woman and Labour*,
1911 (Buchanan-Gould, pp208-209)

Ethnicity

In a global world, definitions of who is African, who
is European, who is American and who is English are
no longer clear. That is one of the reasons why the
world is such an exciting place.

South African writer and journalist **Marianne Thamm**, 'Who's
an African?' 13 February 2002 (*Mental Floss*, 2002, p69)

... what I observe is that ethnicity is being used to
provide platforms from which the amenities of modernity can be competed for. In fact, ethnicity is
beginning to play a perverse role in our political
development. Groups like women, youths, farmers,
traders, workers, interest groups and lobbies are
organizing themselves and trying to articulate and to
protect their interests. The current political atmos-
phere, I must say, is encouraging society to grow ...
but it is threatened by the growth of ethnicity which
we politicians are sometimes promoting for narrow
self-interest.

Winnie Byanyima, Ugandan politician, Proceedings of the
Constituent Assembly, Official Report, 3 August 1994, p1490
(Aili Tripp, University of Wisconsin, 'New Trends in Women's
Political Participation in Africa', presented 27 April 2001

at the Workshop on Democracy in Africa in Comparative Perspective, Stanford University)

'He says,' shouted Van der Merwe, with a wicked glint in his eyes, 'he says that if you come anywhere near his farm, he will throw you all into the river. He says also that he wishes the sea were somewhere near. The river is too good for you damned *uitlanders*.'

South African farmer **Elsa Smithers** describes an Afrikaner farmer's response to a family's request to outspan for the night on his farm (the Afrikaner believed the people were English), *March Hare*, 1935, p131

Exile

In Madagascar when we want to cuddle our babies, we have a song which says, 'Mr. Bird, please take my baby away, and when it stops crying, bring it back.' ... In my song a plane drops me in the jungle in Madagascar amidst all the animals and you can hear in the distance the old lullaby as if my mom is singing it, but she can't hear me, because the forest is so dense. And so we never meet up. The plane is like a big iron bird which has taken me away, but it has never brought me back, which is why I am still crying out there.

Hanitra Rasoanaivo, lead singer of the Malagasy band Tarika, 'Long Way from Home', by Michal Shapiro, www.Rootsworld. com

She no longer asks, no longer argues, she knows: Africa does not want white children. If you have a white skin you can't take shelter anywhere – not even in the south, at its feet. Not any longer. It's best to pack up and find yourself somewhere else to live – before the river bursts its banks.

    Dalene Matthee, South African novelist, *The Day the Swallows Spoke*, 1992, p3

I have left my society for yours without looking back. I have cut my chains and it was fantastic like death.

    Calixthe Beyala, Cameroonian novelist, *Lettre d'une Africaine à ses soeurs occidentals* (iupjournals.org)

I am the immigrant, the exiled star, and I go forward with my head turned back.

    Calixthe Beyala, Cameroonian novelist, *The Little Prince of Belleville* [*Le petite prince de Belleville*], 1992 (iupjournals.org)

I have been denied my home. We have been denied our land ... I am in exile on the outside. We are in exile on the inside.

    Miriam Makeba, South African singer and civil rights activist, *Makeba, My Story*, 1988, p1

Though I have sworn
Never to do the same,
today I saw myself patient
like my mother –
pregnant in a foreign land ...

    Abena P A Busia, Ghanaian poet, opening lines of 'Though I Have Sworn' (Calder, pp21-22)

I have never had a country; not in South Africa or in Botswana.

Bessie Head, South African-born Botswanan writer, *The Best of South African Short Stories*, 1991, p324

Existentialism

'Meaning! Meaning!' I cry out to the Buddhist as I have called out to Dr. Mercer. The good doctor always replied that meaning was the deep comfort of sleep.

Sheila Fugard, South African novelist and poet, *The Castaways*, 1972 (2002 edition, p22)

In a way it is much simpler to take upon oneself a discipline without the consolation of a visionary guide. I believe now that there is no need to find him, the Buddhist, that all I must do is progress in the knowledge of the void, the perennial nothingness of the moment.

Closing lines of the novel *The Castaways*, 1972, by **Sheila Fugard**, South African novelist and poet (2002 edition, p108)

Expatriates

The woman from America loves both Africa and America, independently. She can take what she wants from us both and say: 'Dammit!' It is a difficult thing to do.

Bessie Head, South African-born Botswanan writer, 'The
Woman from America', *Tales of Tenderness and Power*, 1990
(Busby, p486)

Africa belongs to the Africans; the sooner they take
it back the better. But – a country also belongs to
those who feel at home in it.
Doris Lessing, English-Zimbabwean author, *Going Home*,
1968 (Strathern, p499)

'Yes, yes, my dear, in a country like this we all learn
to accept the second-rate.'
Doris Lessing, English-Zimbabwean author, 'Lucy Grange',
The Habit of Loving, 1957 (*The Best of South African Short
Stories*, 1991, p237)

Expendability

On that windy, dust-filled day, where we perched like
miserable birds, and drank our tea, I understood.
We were, all of us simply redundant. If we slipped
off the earth, it would make no difference at all.
Grass would grow ... rocks would stand ... creatures
would find sustenance.
Sheila Fugard, English-South Africa novelist and poet, 'Lace'
(Bruner, *African Women's Writing*, p134)

'Twas one of the gorgeous nights when the sky,
shooting light from a million points, overwhelms
and silences us; and the little circle of our life, that
has seemed to fill all creation, sinks to its proper

size – a shadow, a breath of wind that, being or not being, matters not.

Olive Schreiner, South African writer, *Undine*, 1928 (Emslie, p175)

Sometimes it comforts one so to think what little things we human beings are. It doesn't matter about one's work after all, someone else will do it. That makes one able to be so quiet.

Olive Schreiner, South African writer, letter to Mrs Elizabeth Cobb, 9 January 1885 (Beeton, p84)

Farming

Sure there is oil in Nigeria, and diamonds in Botswana, but growth will come from a strong agriculture-driven economy in almost all places.

Norah Olembu, Kenyan scientist, 'African Scientists Should Become Policy-Makers', *City Press*, 30 November 2003, p43

And the most enticing of the dreams, the unobtainable dreams, was the life of the white farmer, the life of the verandas.

Doris Lessing, English-Zimbabwean writer, 'The Jewel of Africa – Part II', *New York Review of Books*, 10 April 2003

… these new guys, they still think you can farm with a Constitution.

A relative speaking to South African poet and writer **Antjie Krog** in *A Change of Tongue*, 2003, p22

This land, my sister, so begins a song, a song so sad and yet so full of sound and fury. The sound of the women who sweat working on the land and strike the hard earth with their hoes. The fury of working on 'borrowed land' and the fear of being dispossessed looms high above them. They till the land in good times and bad times. They feed the nation. These are the women who will only rest when mother earth claims them back to her and yet in life they never owned the land they slave on.

Ruth Gabi, Zimbabwean writer and teacher, quoted in Getecha, Ciru and Chipika, Jesimen, *Zimbabwe Women's Voices*, 1995, p54 (The African Woman Food Farmer Initiative; www.thp.org)

The drought … was long in breaking. Day after day clouds gathered above the Teniquota Mountains only to fade and melt in the clear bright sky leaving the cold dry air colder and drier than ever. Anxious men, unable to plough till the rains came, spent their days tense and brooding, watching ruin draw slowly nearer.

Pauline Smith, South African writer, 'The Father', *The Little Karoo*, 1925 (1951 reprint, p177)

Fate and Fatalism

Walking alone
With the breaking sea
Crying at our separate fates.

Cesaria Evora, Cape Verdean singer (www.there1.com)

One does not fix appointments with fate.
   Mariama Bâ, Senegalese writer, *So Long a Letter*, 1979 (1981 edition, p2)

Akua my sister,
No one chooses to stand
under a tree in a storm.
   Ama Ata Aidoo, Ghanaian writer, 'Totems' (Chipasula & Chipasula, p51)

Existence is a great pot, and the old Fate who stirs it round cares nothing what rises to the top, and what goes down, and laughs when the bubbles burst.
   Olive Schreiner, South African writer, *The Story of an African Farm*, 1883 (Penguin, 1995, p151)

Fear

I'm not afraid for myself. I have suffered menaces and death threats before. I have lived through the murder of my father, who was the same age as I am now when he died, and the killing of members of my family. Why should I be afraid when so many people in Burundi have died? Anyway, I believe that when your time is up, your time is up.
   Esther Kamatari, Burundian princess and former fashion model, 'Cat-walk Princess Seeks Power in Burundi', by Kim Willsher, 7 November 2004 (www.telegraph.co.uk/news)

Dread attends the unknown.
   Nadine Gordimer, South African writer, *The House Gun*, 1998 (1999 paperback, p6)

When fear comes in the door, logic goes out the window.

Ina Perlman, South African activist, 1994 interview, *Cutting Through the Mountain*, p421

I am a living symbol of whatever is happening in the country. I am a living symbol of the white man's fear.

Winnie Madikizela-Mandela, South African politician and former wife of Nelson Mandela, 'My Little Siberia', *Part of My Soul*, 1984 (Partnow, *The New Quotable Woman*, p449)

I had read of this feeling, how the bigness and silence of Africa, under the ancient sun, grows dense and takes shape in the mind, till even the birds seem to call menacingly, and a deadly spirit comes out of the trees and the rocks. You move warily, as if your very passing disturbs something old and evil, something dark and big and angry that might suddenly rear and strike from behind.

Doris Lessing, English-Zimbabwean author, 'The Old Chief Mshlanga', 1951 (Gardner, p66)

Female Genital Mutilation

… it's wrong and has nothing to do with God. It's something men came up with to keep women under control. Because they can't control themselves, they want us tamed like yard cats. The imams do nothing about it.

Character speaking on female circumcision, **Rayda Jacobs**,
South African author, 'Masquerade', *Post-Cards from South
Africa*, 2004, p22

Why? What was it all for? At that age I didn't understand anything about sex. All I knew was that I had
been butchered with my mother's permission and I
couldn't understand why.

Waris Dirie, Somali supermodel, social activist and writer,
Desert Dawn, 2002 (www.hcc.hawaii.edu)

To be afraid is disgraceful
So much the worse if we die,
We must be brave.

Bangi song before female circumcision (Doob, p23)

Feminism

When we move, we cause ruptures.

Patricia McFadden, scholar and feminist from Swaziland,
'Transformation: An Informal Journal about Yari Yari Pamberi
2004', by Felicia Pride, November 2004 (www.thebacklist.net)

[Womanism is] totality of feminine self-expression,
self-retrieval, and self-assertion in positive cultural
ways.

Mary E Modupe Kolawole, Nigerian academic, *Womanism
and African Consciousness*, Trenton, New Jersey, 1997

There is a relationship between authority in
heaven and authority in the family. I discovered

that unconsciously, when I was a child. This is feminism. Feminism to me, is to understand what are the authorities that are playing and working against you, in heaven or on earth, in the family or in the state? As children we discover that but we are silenced and we are shut up and we are afraid because we are afraid of God.

Nawal El Saadawi, Egyptian writer, psychiatrist and feminist (www.nawalsaadawi.net)

African feminism is perceived by me as MOTHERISM.

Catherine Obianuju Acholonu, Nigerian writer and poet (Bruner, *African Women's Writing*, p186)

A particular feature of the political struggle is the cult that surrounds the wives and widows of imprisoned or killed political leaders. While one has great respect for the women involved, it is telling that it is often only as wife, daughter or mother of Africa that women are accorded significance. I recently heard a prominent woman of great political influence express the view that feminism was a dangerous import and that it was the role of women to be 'the bearers of the future citizens of South Africa'. This echo horrified me, because when I was twelve I heard a Dutch Reform minister say to a group of adolescent Afrikaans girls that 'You are the future mothers of the future sons of Africa.'

Ingrid Fiske, South African poet, 'A Sort of Difference' (Lennox-Short, p206)

To try to remind ourselves and our brothers and lovers and husbands and colleagues that we also exist should not be taken as something foreign, as something bad. African women struggling both on behalf of themselves and on behalf of the wider community is very much a part of our heritage. It is not new and I really refuse to be told I am learning feminism from abroad ...

Ama Ata Aidoo, Ghanaian writer, 'To Be An African Woman Writer', *Criticism and Ideology*, Kirsten Holst Petersen (ed.), Sweden, 1988, p183 (Aidoo, *Changes: A Love Story*, 1991, p172)

Why should a woman not break through conventional restraints that enervate her mind and dwarf her body, and enjoy a wild, free, true life, as a man may? – wander the green world over by the help of hands and feet, and lead a free rough life in bondage to no man? – forget the old morbid loves and longings? – live and enjoy and learn as much as may before the silence comes?

Olive Schreiner, South African writer, *Undine*, 1928 (Emslie, p117)

Foreign Aid

... as a student of economics, she would also try to remember some other truths she knew about Africa. Second-rate experts giving first-class dangerous advice. Or expressing uselessly fifth-rate opinions.

Second-hand machinery from someone else's
junkyard.

Snow plows for tropical farms.
Outmoded tractors.
Discarded aeroplanes.
And now, wigs – made from other people's
unwanted hair.
Ama Ata Aidoo, Ghanaian writer, 'Everything Counts' (Troupe
and Schulte, p35)

As if to justify relief and financial aid, people from
the rich countries are more willing to go to Africa
to implement relief services like feeding emaciated
infants, discover Africans dying of horrible diseases
like AIDs and Ebola, be peacekeepers in war-torn
countries and send horrifying images of tragedies
for television. Hardly any of the friends of Africa are
willing to tackle the political and economic decisions
being made in their own countries and which are
partly responsible for the same horrible images
brought to their living rooms by television. Relevant
questions are deliberately avoided and those who ask
them fall out of favour and become political targets.
Wangari Maathai, Kenyan environmental and human rights
activist, 'Bottle-Necks of Development in Africa', paper
presented at the 4th UN World Women's Conference in
Beijing, China, August-September 1995

Excellent idea ...
How can a
Nigger rule well

Unless his
Balls and purse are
Clutched in
Expert White Hands? . . .

Ama Ata Aidoo, Ghanaian writer, *Our Sister Killjoy or Reflections from a Black-Eyed Squint*, 1979 (Aidoo, *No Sweetness Here*, p154)

Foreign Relations

African needs its Diaspora and the Diaspora needs Africa.

Sokhna Benga, Senegalese scriptwriter and novelist, 'Transformation: An Informal Journal about Yari Yari Pamberi 2004', by Felicia Pride, November 2004 (www.thebacklist.net)

Isn't it clear that the African man alone isn't able to cope without relationship with the West and the rest of the world?

Ama Ata Aidoo, Ghanaian writer (www.kirjasto.sci.fi/aidoo. htm)

The Cold War was not cold in Africa. There, it precipitated some of the most devastating internal wars as African friends and foes of the superpowers fought it out for economic and political control. Support for the wars came from the superpowers and their allies, with much of the support coming in form of aid.

Wangari Maathai, Kenyan environmental and human rights activist, 'Bottle-Necks of Development in Africa,' paper presented at the 4th UN World Women's Conference in Beijing, China, August-September 1995

Diplomats, until they have understood why, always complain that as soon as they understand a country and its language really well, hey presto, off they are whisked to another country. But diplomacy could not continue if the opposing factotums lost a proper sense of national hostility.

Doris Lessing, English-Zimbabwean author, 'Spies I Have Known', *The Story of a Non-Marrying Man and Other Stories*, 1972 (1990 edition, p119)

Forgiveness

Anyway, talking, I tell you, has got to be one of the most effective therapies. A lot of people just need to talk to someone and say: this is what happened to me in my life and I hate myself for it. And all they need to hear is: Hey but that was so many years ago. Forget it.

Lola Shoneyin, Nigerian poet, interview with Nnorom Azuonye, 'My E-conversation with Lola Shoneyin', *Sentinel Poetry*, online magazine, February 2004

... then suddenly there comes that moment, fatal to punier men but a sign of his own future greatness, when he is invaded by sympathy for the enemy.

Doris Lessing, English-Zimbabwean author, 'Spies I Have Known', *The Story of a Non-Marrying Man and Other Stories*, 1972 (1990 edition, p120)

Saints made perfect forgive such injuries, but not a wrinkled woman on the rotten side of forty, with no money or intellect to keep the wine of life from turning sour in her bottle.

Olive Schreiner, South African writer, *Undine*, 1928 (Emslie, p103)

Fortitude and Perseverance

Tomorrow she would think. Now she just had to put one foot in front of the other and keep walking.

Rayda Jacobs, South African author, 'Sabah', *Post-Cards from South Africa*, 2004, p199

This is not a full circle. It's Life carrying on. It's the next breath we all take. It's the choice we make to get on with it.

Alexandra Fuller, British journalist and writer who grew up in Zimbabwe, closing lines of her novel *Don't Let's Go to the Dogs Tonight*, 2003, p310

Aminata can fall, and she will stand up, smiling.

Angélique Kidjo, Beninois musician (www.giantstep.net)

Five years ago in Uganda one man with a gun could walk through the door and take everything you had – just one man with a gun will make you lie down under the table and cover your face, while he takes everything. After you go through an experience like war, you come out a different person. Either you go down with the experience, or you rise, you are enhanced by the experience. So one of the things that the war experience has done for Ugandans is to produce a feeling of getting involved, a feeling of not wanting to suffer under the table.

Woman and AIDS Support Network *Conference Report*, 1990:19 (Kaleeba, p10)

of tonight we shall sleep
to wake many tomorrows
strong, renewed, strong.

Lindiwe Mabuza, South African poet, 'Listening to Mbaqanga' (Troupe and Schulte, p491)

Freedom

Prison taught me that freedom is very important, but it taught me also that I'm ready to lose my freedom ... for a different society. Because, I am not ready to live in a very unjust, oppressive society, and just be free like that ... I will continue to criticize ... even if it keeps me in prison.

Nawal El Saadawi, Egyptian writer, psychiatrist and feminist, 'Nawal el Saadawi – A Creative and Dissident Life', by Brian Belton and Clare Dowding, (www.infed.org)

Pushing someone toward liberty does not set her free; taking the chains off a prisoner does not give him freedom. Freedom was peace.

Ken Bugul, Senegalese writer, *The Abandoned Baobab*, 1984
(English translation 1991, pp70-71)

I see freedom passing from us and the whole land
being grasped by the golden claw.
  Olive Schreiner, South African writer, *Trooper Peter Halket*,
  1897 (Buchanan-Gould, p165)

If the bird *does* like its cage, and *does* like its sugar,
and will not leave it, why keep the door so very
carefully shut?
  Olive Schreiner, South African writer, *The Story of an African
  Farm*, 1883 (Penguin, 1995, p192)

Friendship

There is no such thing as friendship ... we are good
and true and earnest at heart, meaning the best, we
humans, but we cannot understand each other, and
understanding is friendship.
  Olive Schreiner, South African writer, letter to Havelock Ellis,
  1888 (Buchanan-Gould, p96)

Friendship is good, a strong stick; but when the
hour comes to lean hard, it gives. In the day of their
bitterest need, all souls are alone.
  Olive Schreiner, South African writer, *The Story of an African
  Farm*, 1883 (Penguin, 1995, p102)

Future

Every wall is a mountain, and the higher one climbs, the farther one sees into the future.

Ana Paula Taveres, Angolan poet, 'Kuito, A Child's Map of War and Infinity – Photographs and Poetry Regarding Angolan Conflict', *UNESCO Courier*, July 2001

We have to trust that we are going to change. The future will be better, and the lives of children will be better than our lives. And to work on that. That's how I deal with life.

Nawal El Saadawi, Egyptian writer, psychiatrist and feminist, 'Conversation with Dr Nawal el Saadawi', interview by Stephanie McMillan, 1999

In African bidonvilles, everyone has a clear vision of the future. They always speak about tomorrow. For these people, the past and present do not exist. That's crazy. Everything is conjugated in the future tense. 'I'll buy a house.' 'I'll buy a refrigerator.' Never 'I've bought,' always, 'I'll buy.' And this language reflects a moment of loss. Life in the bidonvilles denies the present because one lives on hope. Everyone thinks that they are in transit to a better tomorrow. No one stays there out of sheer pleasure. So you conjugate verbs in the future.

Calixthe Beyala, Cameroonian novelist, interview with Benetta Jules-Rosette, 1998 (Ayo Abiétou Coly, 'Neither Here nor There: Calixthe Beyala's Collapsing Homes', *Research in African Literatures*, Vol. 33, No. 2) (iupjournals.com)

dance with us a dance of the future
they will not let us sit in peace
> **Molara Ogundipe-Leslie**, Nigerian poet, 'Rain at Noon-Time
> (for Julius Nyerere)', 1974 (Chipasula & Chipasula, p100)

Perhaps shadows from the future fall on you as a
warning – perhaps you only turn them into shadows
of foreboding afterwards.
> On premonitions, **Dalene Matthee**, South African novelist,
> *The Day the Swallows Spoke*, 1992, p3

God

God is NOT an individual. And ... woman is half of
God.
> **Kola Boof**, Sudanese-American writer and activist, 'The
> Africana QA: Kola Boof', interview by Jennifer Williams, 18
> May 2004 (Africana website)

All Gods are in danger of falling.
> On the meaning of her name Chimamanda, literally
> translated as 'My God will never fall', **Chimamanda Ngozi
> Adichie**, Nigerian novelist, quoted in 'In the Footsteps of
> Chinua Achebe: Enter Chimamanda Ngozi Adichie, Nigeria's
> Newest Literary Voice', by Ike Anya, *Sentinel Poetry*, online
> magazine, November 2003

God is a woman and women know it and women
keep it quiet, God knows why.
> A favourite saying of Cameroonian playwright **Werewere
> Liking** (Sara Tagliacozzo, 'What Europeans? African Artists'

All of us have a God in us, and that God is the spirit that unites all life, everything that is on this planet.
Wangari Maathai, Kenyan environmental and human rights activist (www.brainyquote.com)

God is inside us, and if god is outside us, it is the collective power of people, when they act, when they revolt against injustice. So god to me is justice. The revolution of people is divine.
Nawal El Saadawi, Egyptian writer, psychiatrist and feminist, 'Conversation with Dr Nawal el Saadawi', interview by Stephanie McMillan, 1999

If you ask me what is my religion, it is hard for me to answer, because we human beings have not framed our speech for the purpose of expressing such thoughts – but if I must put it into words I would say: The Universe is One, and, It Lives; or, if you would put it into older phraseology, I would say: There is NOTHING but God.
Olive Schreiner, South African writer, letter to Reverend M Lloyd (Buchanan-Gould, pp105-106)

Gold

Gold has traditionally been an inflation hedge and a safe haven from turbulent stock markets. But with little inflation and the US Treasury bond the new safe haven, it is no longer a hedge. Gold's no longer precious – it's now just another metal.

Donna Block, South African journalist, 'Between a Rock and the Gold Face', *Mail&Guardian* (South Africa), 11 May 1999

For the poor and despised there is always the idea of gold somewhere else.

Nadine Gordimer, South African writer, 'My Father Leaves Home', *Jump and Other Stories*, 1991, p65

He loved it most at sunset … when the dump became a mountain of gold dust and the dam liquid amber. They could keep their gold bars in their vaults. He was satisfied with the refuse.

Rose Zwi, South African novelist, *Another Year in Africa*, 1980, p17

I that am old have never yet seen a happy man that went digging for gold, or a man that was happy when he had found it. Surely it is sin and sorrow that drives men to it, and sin and sorrow that comes to them from it.

Pauline Smith, South African writer, 'The Schoolmaster', *The Little Karoo*, 1925 (1951 reprint, pp43-44)

The gold they have fought for will divide them, till they slay one another over it.

Olive Schreiner, South African writer, 'Eighteen Ninety-nine', Hanover, Cape Colony (South Africa), 1905 (Clayton, p113)

Gold is like charity; it covers a multitude of sins …

Olive Schreiner, South African writer, *Undine*, 1928 (Emslie, p40)

Goodness

You owe me nothing. You're a good person. Good people don't owe one another anything – we are one another.

Dalene Matthee, South African novelist, *The Day the Swallows Spoke*, 1992, p263

The good child who willingly goes on errands eats the food of peace.

Ama Ata Aidoo, Ghanaian writer, 'The Late Bud', *No Sweetness Here*, 1970 (1995 edition, p103)

We can work together for a better world with men and women of goodwill, those who radiate the intrinsic goodness of humankind.

Wangari Maathai, Kenyan environmental and human rights activist (www.brainyquote.com)

It is better to be ugly and good than pretty and bad; though of course it's nice when one is both.

Olive Schreiner, South African writer, *The Story of an African Farm*, 1883 (Penguin, 1995, p74)

Governance

The state of any country's environment is a reflection of the kind of governance in place, and without good governance there can be no peace.

Wangari Maathai, Kenyan environmental and human rights activist, Nobel Lecture after receiving the Nobel Peace Prize, Oslo, Norway, 10 December 2004

The recent power sharing in South Africa offers an interesting alternative for Africa. Everything notwithstanding, the dominant political culture of 'winner takes all' was forfeited for national unity in an experiment which however, awaits the test of time. South Africans have enormous mountains to climb and it is prudent to see how they will accomplish the feat ... the South African experiment ... offers an interesting alternative approach to power as Africa continues the search for good governance in the African context.

Wangari Maathai, Kenyan environmental and human rights activist, 'Bottle-Necks of Development in Africa', paper presented at the 4th UN World Women's Conference in Beijing, China, August-September 1995

Government

She couldn't be really grateful to our President! What would she be thanking him for? For heading a government that makes policies which tighten the noose around the neck of the common man? ... Could it be for essential services which don't work? Or, a runaway inflation which defies solution? Was she being grateful for the constant upward review of the prices of petroleum products which in turn, raises the cost of living? Is she grateful for the permanent bad state of our roads, non-existent medical care, poor transport system, poor health and educational services? Or the dwindling value of our currency, or the upsurge in crime which makes it impossible for Nigerians to feel safe within or outside their homes?

> **Helen Ovbiagele**, Nigerian writer and editor, 'That Mother's Gratitude to the Government', *Vanguard*, 26 December 2004

Government has no business being in business.

> **Ellen Johnson-Sirleaf**, Liberian banker and politician (Patricia A Made, 'Africa's First Woman President?', *Inter Press Service*, 18 July 1997)

No one ever gets it perfectly right, and certainly not governments.

> **Gill Marcus**, South African politician, 1995 interview, *Cutting Through the Mountain*, p264

The government of the world was [Cecil] Rhodes' simple desire.

> **Sarah Gertrude Millin**, South African writer (quotes.liberty-tree.ca)

Grief and Trauma

So long as nobody moved, nobody uttered, the word and the act within the word could not enter here.

Nadine Gordimer, South African writer, *The House Gun*, 1998
(1999 paperback, p5)

... time passes and grief stands still ...
Sheila Fugard, South African novelist and poet, *The Castaways*, 1972 (2002 edition, p17)

Some of her children die every day, and nature might go about for ever in deep weeds and mourning if she took the trouble to lament for them; so she goes on smiling, though the best-loved and the dearest have just gone – smiling, smiling, when our hearts are breaking. Why should the sky be clouded and the birds fly home hungry, because in one small tent a man lay stiff and white? Men whom women's hearts had yearned over died just so every week, and the world rushed on the same.
Olive Schreiner, South African writer, *Undine*, 1929
(Buchanan-Gould, p49)

Guilt

As benefactors of the old regime, whites were shot through with guilt. And where there was guilt there was opportunity.
Rayda Jacobs, South African author, 'The Guilt', *Post-Cards from South Africa*, 2004, p130

'When does the struggle come to an end? When can one start living without feeling guilty because

you want to be happy? When does one get to *life*,
Father?'

Dalene Matthee, South African novelist, *The Day the Swallows
Spoke*, 1992, p58

Hair

Second to skin, black people's hair has been historically devalued as the most visible stigmata of black-
ness. While formalized race science was not central
to apartheid, ideas of racial hierarchy are central to
South African history and experience. In modern
South African urban social circles, the way one keeps
their hair has become a convenient way to categor-
ize people, and, in our search for an African Identity
that connects us to the rest of the continent, we
have become stuck on the notion that our hair
makes us who we are.

Gabi Ngcobo, South African artist, quoted in 'Young, Black,
and Gifted Womyn', by Muholi Z, *Behind the Mask* website, 26
January 2004

'And your hair? What do you do with that bush?'
'Some perfectly sensible people,' I reply, 'pay pounds
to turn their sleek hair into precisely such a bushy
tangle.'

Zoë Wicomb, South African writer, 'A Trip to the Gifberge',
1987 (Medalie, p130)

Why should we take off the hair of our body? Many fundamentalists in Arab regions want women to cover their hairs, why? What is the problem with the hair of the women? Because hair is power. Hair is power. When they put people in prison, they shave them. Hair is an organism, it is a living organism, and it is part of you. My hair covers my head; it protects my head also. That is why it is natural. Hair is a natural organ in your body. Why should you hide it, why should you dye it? Why should you shave it?

Nawal El Saadawi, Egyptian writer, psychiatrist and feminist, 'Empowerment of Women, Writing and Fighting', lecture, 1981

I see other black women imitate my style, which is no style at all, but just letting your hair be itself. They call it the 'Afro Look'.

Miriam Makeba, South African singer and civil rights activist, 1960s (www.unhcr-50.org/gallery)

Happiness

Now, having seen it for myself because of my Babamukuru's kindness, I too could think of planting things for merrier reasons than the chore of keeping breath in the body. I wrote it down in my head: I would ask Maiguru for some bulbs and plant a bed of those gay lilies on the homestead. In front of the house. Our home would answer well to being cheered up by such lively flowers. Bright and cheery, they had been planted for joy. What a strange idea that was. It was a liberation ...

Tsitsi Dangarembga, Zimbabwean writer, *Nervous Conditions*, 1988, p64

The word 'happiness' does indeed have meaning, doesn't it? I shall go out in search of it.

Mariama Bâ, Senegalese writer, *So Long a Letter*, 1979 (1981 edition, p89)

To rush the world over seeking for happiness is a fool's work.

Olive Schreiner, South African writer, *Undine*, 1928 (Emslie, p132)

Hate

Then, life dealt me and my people such stinking cards. I had to struggle very hard to chase hatred out of my heart – to say 'get out, there is no room for you here!'

Gcina Mhlope, South African writer and actress, 'Jozi-Jozi, City of Dreams', *From Jo'burg to Jozi*, 2002, p171

Today, one can say that South Africa is hate-free ... Anybody who would want to express naked hatred would feel somehow humble, humiliated and full of guilt to descend to hate while Mandela, after what he went through personally, has forgiven so much.

Nadine Gordimer, South African writer, article in Kenya's
Daily Nation, 16 June 1999

If you want to destroy a man, teach him to hate
himself; if you want to destroy a people, get the
children to hate themselves.

Dalene Matthee, South African novelist, *The Day the Swallows
Spoke*, 1992, p98

Am I hating because I do not want to understand?

Sheila Fugard, South African novelist and poet, *The
Castaways*, 1972 (2002 edition, p18)

History

It frustrates me that we chose, in Nigeria, to ignore
our recent history. I am often asked why I write
about Biafra, as though it is something I have to
justify … We do not just risk repeating history if we
sweep it under the carpet, we also risk being myopic
about our present.

Chimamanda Ngozi Adichie, Nigerian novelist, quoted in 'In
the Footsteps of Chinua Achebe: Enter Chimamanda Ngozi
Adichie, Nigeria's Newest Literary Voice', by Ike Anya, *Sentinel
Poetry*, online magazine, November 2003

I really believe quite strongly that if the history of
the 20th century teaches us anything, it's the re-
examination of our heroes. I would never deny that
my parents played an absolutely heroic role in the

anti-apartheid struggle. But they were also human beings. And if we cannot allow our heroes to be human beings, we're in serious trouble.

> **Gillian Slovo**, writer and daughter of South African anti-apartheid activists Joe Slovo and Ruth First, 'Daughter of the Struggle', *Salon*, June 1997 (www.salon.com)

'My dear young man,' said the visiting professor, 'to give you the decent answer your anxiety demands, I would have to tell you a detailed history of the African continent. And to do that, I shall have to speak every day, twenty-four hours a day, for at least three thousand years. And I don't mean to be rude to you or anything, but who has that kind of time?'

> **Ama Ata Aidoo**, Ghanaian writer, *Our Sister Killjoy*, 1977

How ridiculous is it to teach children only the history of their own little countries … We make so little effort to make education broad … What a farce to spend time gaining a little dry smattering of the grammar of a foreign language and to know nothing of its literature or the history of the nation …

> **Olive Schreiner**, South African writer, writing in a letter (Buchanan-Gould, p200)

HIV/AIDS

Apartheid taught us how to manoeuvre in denial.

> On AIDS, **Lebogang Mashile**, South African poet,

'Transformation: An Informal Journal about Yari Yari Pamberi 2004', by Felicia Pride, November 2004 (www.thebacklist.net)

The first and most important thing has been to educate Africans about the disease, so that they address it from a point of information, rather than from a point of ignorance and fear. And the other is to provide medicine for those who are unfortunate enough to be infected. And probably, the third is to address the issue of poverty, which is one cause of – not infection – but rather the cause of death. Because many Africans in their poverty, they do not have adequate immune systems, and therefore, when they are infected they succumb to the virus very quickly.

Wangari Maathai, Kenyan environmental and human rights activist, interviewed by Marika Griehsel, after being awarded the Nobel Peace Prize, 8 October 2004

It's a health issue of course at one level but it's also a gender issue because one of the reasons that we see such high levels of infection is that women still are unable to really negotiate sex on an equal basis with men. Women find they are pressured to have children when they don't want to have children. Women remain in abusive relationships because they feel that part of being female is to define themselves in terms of a male partner. Therefore if you step out you have failed as a woman, you've failed your family. So there is still a lot of pressure to remain in those relationships. And one of the main ways of stopping HIV infection is the use of condoms, and women, unless they [are] equal to be able to negotiate that relationship, they can't really demand the use of condoms.

Unity Dow, High Court Judge of Botswana, interview with Ian Henschke of the Australian Broadcasting Corporation, 3 October 2004

I was angry at God, I thought God had treated me unfairly, I felt betrayed because I had done everything a housewife and a mother should do. I felt my family did not deserve this.

On her reaction upon learning in 1987 that her husband Christopher had AIDS, **Noerine Kaleeba**, Ugandan HIV/AIDS activist, 'Noerine Kaleeba, the Brain Behind TASO', by Joe Nam, *New Vision* (Kampala), 5 April 2004

There is a risk in challenging cultural taboos. But there is a greater risk of losing the whole of our population.

Simone Ehivet Gbagbo, first lady of Côte d'Ivoire, speaking to the summit of first ladies from 10 African nations in Rwanda, 'Africa's First Ladies Discuss Strategies To Combat Spread Of HIV/AIDS', Sapa-AP, 21 May 2001

It's hard to worry about something that is going to kill you one day when so many other problems are going to kill you tomorrow.

Ruth Labode, Zimbabwean medical doctor (Michael Specter, 'Zimbabwe's Descent Into AIDS Abyss: Little Hope, Much Despair', *The New York Times*, 6 August 1998)

We are a culture that knows about death, but we don't discuss it. We don't discuss sex either. With us, you can have sex as long as you don't let us know. There is a whole language for discussing sex, but it is very subtle – a child could be in the room and would never know that is what you are talking about. But a person who has AIDS, every time you look at this person you must confront sex and death. These are the things that make it too difficult to handle.

Noerine Kaleeba, Ugandan working for UNAIDS (Suzanne Daley, 'AIDS Is Everywhere, But the Africans Look Away', *The New York Times*, 4 December 1998)

It is wickedly selfish and ironic that, the use of a simple sheath, with no known health hazards will literally save lives; and this simple remedy is subject to the whims of mere men.

Nana Ama Amamoo, senior programme officer, Akina Mama wa Africa, excerpt from a paper presented at an HIV/AIDS conference in London, September 1995 ('Working with Men for Change: Gender and HIV Prevention in the African Community in the UK', pamphlet)

AIDS has brought two major taboos – death and sex – to the dining table.

Noerine Kaleeba, Director of The HIV/AIDS Support Organization, Uganda, *The Herald*, Harare, Zimbabwe, 18 October 1990 (Kaleeba, p59)

Hope

There is power in hope.

> **Nawal El Saadawi**, Egyptian writer, psychiatrist and feminist, 'Transformation: An Informal Journal about Yari Yari Pamberi 2004', by Felicia Pride, November 2004 (www.thebacklist.net)

Is there hope for the African woman?
Will next century meet her asleep?

> From the poem 'African Woman' by Cameroonian social activist **Grace Eneme**, quoted in 'Women Standing up to Adjustment in Africa', report of the African Women's Economic Policy Network, July 1996 (The African Woman Food Farmer Initiative; www.thp.org)

I know there will be spring; as surely as the birds know it when they see above the snow two tiny, quivering green leaves. Spring cannot fail us.

> **Olive Schreiner**, South African writer, 'The Woman's Rose', Matjiesfontein, South Africa, 1890-1891 (Clayton, p61)

Hopelessness

Ateba gives her a sidelong glance and vaguely suggests an abortion. After all what does one kid's life matter in a country where everything is constantly in an embryonic state? The kids will always be skinny and never have an opportunity to grow sturdy.

> **Calixthe Beyala**, Cameroonian novelist, *Your Name Shall Be Tanga* [*Tu t'appelleras Tanga*], 1988 (iupjournals.org)

How do you live in a country that goes along upside down? Turn towards the sky? It remains obstinately silent. The men get drunk on jojoba and do their utmost blasphemes against a forgetful god. Prisoners, caught within the barbed wire of tradition, the women roam around the muck-filled streets, forever and always following the sex organs that tear them to pieces. As for the children, they let death take them away, grown old from having pounded too many manioc leaves to feed their parents.

Calixthe Beyala, Cameroonian novelist, *Your Name Shall Be Tanga* [*Tu t'appelleras Tanga*], 1988 (iupjournals.org)

Humanity

Africa is the cradle of humanity, and if humanity forgets its cradle then it deserves to perish.

Kovambo Nujoma, first lady of Namibia, Conference of African First Ladies on HIV/AIDS, Geneva, 17-19 July 2002

There's only own humankind – I believe that to my gut. The reason I believe this so strongly is because I was raised in Africa, and if you are raised in nature, you understand and respect every life. That's something that some people try to keep away from one another, because once you understand that, there's no need to hate anybody any more. There's no need to say 'they' and 'we' – we are all one.

Angélique Kidjo, Beninois musician (www.giantstep.net)

I believe in the benign nature of human beings. I don't believe that people are inheriting this malignant, un-divine nature. I think we are born in a very benign good nature, a human nature, but we lose our humanity because of political systems.

Nawal El Saadawi, Egyptian writer, psychiatrist and feminist, quoted in 'Nawal el Saadawi – A Creative and Dissident Life', by Brian Belton and Clare Dowding (www.infed.org)

To me, it underlined the basic tragedy of the human race – that basically we are not very nice, are we? Power only corrupts if you are not intrinsically good.

Ina Perlman, South African activist, 1994 interview, *Cutting Through the Mountain*, p407

The knowledge that one is not alone ... that the struggle is an international struggle for the dignity of man, and that you are part of this family of man, this alone sustains you.

Winnie Madikizela-Mandela, South African politician and former wife of Nelson Mandela (Amoah, p132)

Man is one: greatness and animal fused together. None of his acts is pure charity. None is pure bestiality.

Mariama Bâ, Senegalese writer, *So Long a Letter*, 1979 (1981 edition, p32)

The fact that human beings, given half a chance, start seeing each other's points of view seems to me the only ray of hope there is for humanity ...

Doris Lessing, English-Zimbabwean author, 'Spies I Have Known', *The Story of a Non-Marrying Man and Other Stories*, 1972 (1990 edition, p119)

It seems to me more and more that the only thing that really matters in life is not wealth or poverty, pleasure or hardship, but the nature of the human beings with whom one is thrown into contact, and one's relation to them.

Olive Schreiner, South African writer, *Letters*, 1924 (Buchanan-Gould, p193)

Hunger

There can be no sustainable democracy when people are hungry and poor. In my view, hunger and poverty are as dehumanizing as political oppression.

Nkosazana Dlamini-Zuma, South African Minister of Foreign Affairs (*Great South Africans*, 2004, p208)

Food has even become a political weapon with leaders in power keeping the key to the national granaries, disposing of the food even when their own people need it and subsequently appealing for food from the international community ... only a government which cares about its people will protect its citizens from the politics of food.

Wangari Maathai, Kenyan environmental and human rights activist, 'Bottle-Necks of Development in Africa', paper presented at the 4th UN World Women's Conference in Beijing, China, August-September 1995

Hunger is beating me.
Bread is common, gold is rare; but the hungry man
will barter all your mines for one morsel of bread.

Olive Schreiner, South African writer, *The Story of an African Farm*, 1883 (Penguin, 1995, p187)

Idealism

I do not glorify the great ideal, the Ethiopian woman
    that I see,
I glorify that simple jet-skinned soul, the Mother of
    the coloured race to be,
Because she fought through danger and cried shame
    unto those
Who trample in the sod humanity; she should be
    glorified.

Gladys Casely-Hayford, Ghanaian-Sierra Leonean poet, 'The Ideal' (Busby, p219)

You cannot capture the ideal by a coup d'état.

Olive Schreiner, South African writer, title of chapter eight of her novel *From Man to Man*, 1927 (Emslie, p545)

Identity

In the midst of the ochre dunes, among the vast expanses of golden sand, in the palm groves inhabited by the Blue Men, I realized where my roots lay. I am Moroccan through and through, to the core of my being.

But I also feel very French, through the language, my culture, mentality and intellect. The two are no longer incompatible. In me, East and West at last cohabit in peace.

Malika Oufkir, Moroccan heiress imprisoned with her family for twenty years, and Michèle Fitoussi, *Stolen Lives, Twenty Years in a Desert Jail*, 1999, p288

Like the street names that have been removed for their Eurocentricity, my parents and their friends are displaced. They do not understand the new signs. Their silhouettes glide across the garden, outlining their nostalgia.

Maureen Isaacson, South African writer and journalist, 'Holding Back Midnight', 1992 (Medalie, p154)

Coloureds haven't been around for that long, perhaps that's why we stray. Just think, in our teens we wanted to be white, now we want to be full-blooded Africans. We've never wanted to be ourselves and that's why we stray ... across the continent, across the oceans ...

Zoë Wicomb, South African writer, *You Can't Get Lost in Cape Town*, 1987 (Bharati Mukherjee, 'They Never Wanted to Be Themselves', *The New York Times*, 24 May 1987)

She will have to be burnt in all the suns, all the fires of desire, customs and the most oppressive, outmoded traditions before she is finally able to discover herself.

Calixthe Beyala, Cameroonian novelist, back cover of *It is the*

Sun Which Has Burnt Me [*C'est le soleil qui m'a brûlée*], 1987
(www.arts.uwa.edu.au)

... self-knowledge comes too late
and by the time I've known myself
I am no longer what I was.
> **Mabel Segun**, Nigerian poet, first stanza of 'The Pigeon-Hole'
> (Busby, p372)

tortured and magnificent
proud and mysterious
Africa from head to foot
This is what I am.
> **Noémia de Sousa**, Mozambican poet, 'If You Want to Know
> Me', *When Bullets Begin to Flower*, 1972, translated by
> Margaret Dickinson (Busby, p329)

Infidelity

He struck and I slipped to the floor ... then I heard
him, as if echoing from within a prison cell in
which he found himself, in which he wrestled, in
which he was trying to keep me. From inside this
nightmare space, inside this bodily fear, my eyes
closed, and hidden under my arms, under my lifted
elbows, under my already bloody hands, I heard and
I would almost have answered with a laugh, not a
madwoman's laugh nor one of tearfulness, but the
laugh of a woman who was relieved and struggling
to free herself. 'Adulteress!' he repeated, 'Anywhere,

except this city of iniquity, you would deserve to be stoned!'

Assia Djebar, Algerian novelist, *So Vast the Prison*, 1995 (www.amazon.com)

You may ask, did I not know that sometimes after men and women had married they might find they had made a mistake, that, however loyal and true was the love they had given, they might find some human creature who might have been more to them than the one they married?

And I answer, yes, I had thought of this; it had seemed to me the great attendant tragedy that waits on human marriage.

Olive Schreiner, South African writer, *From Man to Man*, 1927 (Emslie, p554)

Intelligence

If you have no thought of your own, those of other men will find nothing to which they can fasten themselves.

Olive Schreiner, South African writer, *Undine*, 1928 (Emslie, p47)

The less a woman has in her head the lighter she is for climbing. I once heard an old man say, that he never saw intellect help a woman so much as a pretty ankle.

Olive Schreiner, South African writer, *The Story of an African Farm*, 1883 (Penguin, 1995, p189)

Islam

They're staunch, I'll give them that. The worst one
will fast during the holy month. But they have a
pride, especially on Fridays when they get two hours
for lunch to attend mosque, and in Ramadan when
they're fasting. They'll sit there with their parched
lips and stiff smiles showing you how your biscuits
and tea don't affect them, and you just know they
think they're closer to God.

   Rayda Jacobs, South African author, 'Give Them Too Much',
   Post-Cards from South Africa, 2004, p89

Islam, like Christianity, is a foreign religion forced
upon North Africans through enslavement. I
experienced it to be a misogynist religion that
catered to hatred and violence against women.
Neither I, nor the sons of my womb shall stand for
it, but since I am not God, I will respect and support
other people's right to choose the Islamic and
Christian religions.

   Kola Boof, Sudanese-American writer and activist, 'The
   Africana QA: Kola Boof', interview by Jennifer Williams, 18
   May 2004 (Africana website)

Surely, if we can stone a woman for having sex
without a husband, then we can also suspend a
stupid boys club (Islam) that caters to men's most
ancient insecurities and offers up to the world
nothing but violence and macho segregation, and as
an African woman born Muslim, that's all Islam is in

my opinion. It should be abolished. And so should
Christianity, Judaism and every other religion that
the men created. But that's just Kola Boof's opinion.

Kola Boof, Sudanese-American writer and activist, press
statement, 3 January 2003 (www.kolaboof.com)

Journalism

Anyone who has worked on a newspaper would
have to admit that some of what ends up under the
grand banner of journalism is thoughtless rubbish.

Charlotte Bauer, South African journalist, 'Opinion:
Plagiarism Isn't Ambiguous; It's Just Theft, Plain And Simple',
Sunday Times (Johannesburg), 7 February 2005

I have observed in Africa how Western journalists
are drawn towards what I call the '3 D's': Disease,
Deprivation and Despair ... They are not interested
in anything else – in fact they actually avert their
eyes from signs of progress or modernization, or
evidence of plain, everyday normality: precisely
the kind of stories they would go for in their own
countries. They don't want to know. If it's Africa, it's
got to be abnormal!

Stella Orakwue, Nigerian journalist, *New African*, July/August,
2001

In a day and age where anyone can anonymously
fax, e-mail and post in the internet anything,
people in our community who are engaged in

the honourable and mostly thankless service of journalism should be especially vigilant in the way they process information they receive regarding other people. Not only should they rigorously ascertain the credibility of their sources, but they should also make every effort to report on differing view points as well.

> Ethiopian singer **Aster Aweke**, interview in *Ethiopian Review*, July 1997 (ethiopianreview.homestead.com)

Judaism

By not aligning yourself with the oppressed you are betraying the Jewish tradition.

> **Pauline Podbrey**, South African trade unionist, 1994 interview, *Cutting Through the Mountain*, p70

Then Mom started mourning softly, but loud enough to be heard, that she wished Jessica had found a nice English or Afrikaans boy instead of causing complications. Finally, Billy, incensed, shouted that there were no more if onlies; marriage came suddenly.

> Excerpt from a short story describing the wedding day of a Christian woman and a Jewish man, **Sheila Roberts**, South African writer, 'The Wedding', 1973 (*The Best of South African Short Stories*, 1991, p360)

She herself much valued her strain of Jewish blood, and used to tell with laughter how once, in a large Cape Town store, she saw coming towards her a shabby little Jewess. 'My heart went out to her, and then I bumped my nose in the large mirror!'

Lyndall Gregg, writing about her aunt, South African writer Olive Schreiner, *Memories of Olive Schreiner*, 1957, p70

Justice and Injustice

Judge, what were you thinking?

Title of a CD by the Algerian women's group '**20 Ans Barakat**' (www.globalfundforwomen.org, 2004)

The business of keeping people locked up without trial is the absolute death knell to the system of justice.

Helen Suzman, South African parliamentarian (*Great South Africans*, 2004, p100)

Today who can deny that justice is not to be found anywhere in our globe, that it is absent in both the international and national affairs of the world? Who can deny that freedom and democracy are absent from our personal and public lives, that human massacres continue to take thousands of innocent lives, that terror and violence have spread over the East and West.

Nawal El Saadawi, Egyptian writer, psychiatrist and feminist, 'Towards a Philosophy that will Awaken the Conscience of the Human Race', paper for the 6th International Conference of the Arab Women's Solidarity Association, Cairo, 3-5 January 2002

My present sense about the legal aspect of dealing with offenders is that the law remain a guardian and protector of Society and should not be confused with personal forgiveness. However in bringing justice to bear it should be in restorative ways, through paying back to society a debt, rather than punitive. This may be difficult and costly, but may be the only way to model the protection of human rights – rather than perpetuate human rights violation.

Ginn Fourie, South African professor, whose daughter Lyndi was killed by anti-apartheid soldiers in the Heidelberg Tavern attack in Cape Town in 1993

Words are walls I cannot see through. I don't even know what justice or injustice is any more; I no longer believe in either of them. What are the masses shouting for? Is it freedom, or is it simply the right to live in a state of anarchy?

Dalene Matthee, South African novelist, *The Day the Swallows Spoke*, 1992, p145

She felt it was an unjust world this, in which one woman wins all the cakes and bon-bons and another nothing more than dry bread and weak tea.

Olive Schreiner, South African writer, *Undine*, 1928 (Emslie, p88)

Land

Pulling away from the ground causes death by suffocation, starvation. That's what the people of this land believe. Deprive us of the land and you are depriving us of air, water, food, and sex.

Alexandra Fuller, British journalist and writer who grew up in Zimbabwe, *Don't Let's Go to the Dogs Tonight*, 2003, p154

Land is immortal, for it harbours the mysteries of creation.

Expression of the **grandmother of Anwar el-Sadat**, third president of Egypt, *In Search of Identity*, 1978, p3

The poor white here, though he belongs to the soil, has no roots in the soil. He is by nature a wanderer, with none of that conservative love of place which makes to so many men one spot on earth beloved above all others.

Pauline Smith, South African writer, 'Desolation' (Dodd, p51)

Language

It's great to be bilingual, but it's shit to have a language that you can't use anywhere else.

On Afrikaans, **Charlize Theron**, South African actress, 'Out of Africa', Emma Brockes, *The Guardian*, 2 April 2004 (http://film.guardian.co.uk)

Listen, mate, get this and get it fast: English, unlike Portuguese, is no longer a colonial language; it is the language of international business. You wanna teach that in your schools.

Stella Orakwue, Nigerian journalist, 'Angola: A Country in Deepest Transition', *New African*, January 2003, p54

Language is used to mystify and mislead people.

Nawal El Saadawi, Egyptian writer, psychiatrist and feminist, 'Towards a Philosophy that will Awaken the Conscience of the Human Race', paper presented at the 6th International Conference of the Arab Women's Solidarity Association, Cairo, 3-5 January 2002

Igbo is my emotional language. English sounds colourless and grey in translation. Igbo uses colourful phrases, and the language itself will always remain closest to my heart.

Buchi Emecheta, Nigerian writer, interview with Julie Holmes, *The Voice*, 9 July 1996

Insisting on foreign languages for universal functional literacy in Africa is tragic because literacy, use of own language and culture are very important in human development and in cultivating self-worth, self-confidence and self-pride ... How proud would the English be if they were forced to speak French or German and vice versa? Why should Africans be different?

Wangari Maathai, Kenyan environmental and human rights activist, 'Bottle-Necks of Development in Africa', paper presented at the 4th UN World Women's Conference in Beijing, China, August-September 1995

These missionaries, the strange ones, liked to speak Shona much more than they liked to speak English. And when you, wanting to practise your English, spoke to them in English, they always answered in Shona. It was disappointing, and confusing too for people like me who were bilingual ...

Tsitsi Dangarembga, Zimbabwean writer, *Nervous Conditions*,
1988, p104

I know his lingo, too, fairly well. That's the only
thing that'll bring you near a native. And they don't
seem so queer when you have their speech and
know where they come from.

Ethelreda Lewis, South African writer, 'Blind Justice', 1920s
(Dodd, p86)

Leadership

Entire communities ... come to understand that
while it is necessary to hold their governments
accountable, it is equally important that in their
own relationships with each other, they exemplify
the leadership values they wish to see in their own
leaders, namely justice, integrity and trust.

Professor **Wangari Maathai**, Kenyan environmental and
human rights activist, Nobel Lecture after receiving the Nobel
Peace Prize, Oslo, Norway, 10 December 2004

When are we going to get out of the woods in this
country? Not as long as men continue to rule. What
do they know about human welfare when they're so
keen on making decisions which ruin human lives
all over the world?

Helen Ovbiagele, Nigerian writer and editor, 'That Mother's
Gratitude to the Government', *Vanguard*, 26 December 2004

You have to play the mother chicken which provides refuge for everybody. You must be a tower of hope, a model and a motivator. It also takes patience as one has to take all the insults and intimidation because a lot of people will say that you are too assertive.

Sarah Jibril, Nigerian politican, on what it takes to be a female politician in Nigeria, 'The Essential Sarah Jibril', interview with Josephine Lohor, *ThisDay Online*, 16 November 2004

Our leaders are not in the habit of listening to the truth or wise counsel.

Lola Shoneyin, Nigerian poet, interview with Nnorom Azuonye, 'My E-conversation with Lola Shoneyin', *Sentinel Poetry*, online magazine, February 2004

Women must rise above being good managers – of the man, the home, the children and all things spicy and sweet – and boldly step out into visionary leadership.

Lucy Oriang, Kenyan journalist, writing in Nairobi's *Daily Nation* ('Charity Ngilu: Kenya's Leading Woman, by Sarah Coleman, July 2003 issue of *World Press Review*, Vol. 50, No. 7)

If you want to develop Africa, you must develop the leadership of African women.

Soukeyna Ba, President of Women's Development Enterprise in Dakar, Senegal (The African Woman Food Farmer Initiative; www.thp.org)

Liberia [is] a country whose fate and progress have been placed in the hands of many idiots.

Ellen Johnson-Sirleaf, Liberian banker and politician (Ayittey, p197)

If there is a Gandhi in Kenya, he has not come forward.

Wangari Maathi, Kenyan environmental and human rights activist (John Stackhouse, 'Kenya Slides Into Turmoil', *The Globe and Mail*, November 1995)

Africa has suffered from lack of enlightened leadership and a bad style of political and economic guidance. While African leaders could have excused themselves for being unable to protect their people from the exploits of colonial empires in the l9th and 20th centuries, they can hardly escape blame for allowing neo-colonial exploitation which continues to reduce many of their people into paupers in their own countries.

Wangari Maathai, Kenyan environmental and human rights activist, 'Bottle-Necks of Development in Africa', paper presented at the 4th UN World Women's Conference in Beijing, China, August-September 1995

If, like men around the world, African men harbour any phobias about women moving into leadership positions, then they had better get rid of them quickly ...

Ama Ata Aidoo, Ghanaian writer ('The African Woman Today', *Dissent*, Summer 1992)

... he's bombastic and rabble-rousing and he drinks and he whores around. He'll probably be the first

Prime Minister – he has all the qualities – the common touch, you know.

Doris Lessing, English-Zimbabwean author, *The Golden Notebook*, 1962 (Bloom, p54)

I do not enjoin my daughter who will inherit me on the throne to become a god for her people who draws her authority over her people from the divinity of gods, but I enjoin her to be a just and compassionate ruler.

Noot, ancient Egyptian god of the sky to her daughter Isis, 4988 BC ('Towards a Philosophy that will Awaken the Conscience of the Human Race', Nawal El Saadawi, January 2002)

Liberation

I will be happy for the day when the women of the earth realize once more that it is an abomination against God for any woman's breasts to be covered. And that a woman's menstrual cycle is to be celebrated, because that is how humans come upon the earth. Through woman.

Kola Boof, Sudanese-American writer and activist, press statement, 3 January 2003 (www.kolaboof.com)

Women don't have to shout for their rights or their empowerment when they are able to be economically independent; then these come automatically.

Lucia Quachey, President of the African Federation of Women Entrepreneurs, quoted in Snyder, Margaret C and Tadesse, Mary, *African Women and Development*, 1995, pp183-4 (The African Woman Food Farmer Initiative; www.thp.org)

Oh my friend, disaster has rung my doorbell. The women have gutted themselves behind my back. They've taken off their pagnes and dressed themselves anew in muslin. Nothing is called by its name anymore. I no longer recognize the geography of the land drawn in MY OWN HOUSE ... And they take the initiative. They make love to me and I'm ashamed. Since when friend, and in what country do women govern? ... Nostalgia exhausts me and tears me apart ... Me, I am lost.

Calixthe Beyala, Cameroonian novelist, *The Little Prince of Belleville* [*Le petit prince de Belleville*], 1992 (iupjournals.org)

African women in general need to know that it's OK for them to be the way they are – to see the way they are as a strength, and to be liberated from fear and from silence.

Wangari Maathai, Kenyan environmental and human rights activist (www.brainyquote.com)

Lifting her eyes to the certainty of victory,
Knowing that victory was built through sacrifice –
Who is it?
She who lifts high the beacon of freedom,
Who cries to the whole world
That our struggle is the same –
It's the emancipated Mozambican woman
Who brings her courage to the People.

'Song of the Mozambican Woman' (Searle, pp44-45)

Life

I can enjoy anywhere, and I can leave it. Life is about moving on.

Waris Dirie, Somali supermodel, social activist and writer, 'Somalia's Desert Flower', by Helen Gibson, *Time Europe* magazine, 15 July 2002

When we lead small lives we become small people.

South African writer and journalist **Marianne Thamm**, 'Give me the real thing', 23 May 2001 (*Mental Floss*, 2002, p21)

I cannot be in the position I'm in and expect everything to be wonderful. It's life, and some things are good. It's like one day chicken, next day feathers.

Sade, Nigerian singer, interview with Lonnae O'Neal Parker, *Essence*, March 2001

You make a contribution to others. That to me is a life of value.

Gill Marcus, South African politician, 1995 interview, *Cutting Through the Mountain*, p265

beat out your own rhythms
and rhythms of your life
but make the song soulful
and make life
sing

Micere Githae Mugo, Kenyan poet, 'Where Are Those Songs' (Busby, p552)

Life has a way of catching you unaware. Suddenly a year has gone by or many years and you hadn't noticed it. Suddenly you realize that your hair has grown white and you hadn't noticed it. Or that another life is being planned; unseen activities which touch upon your life, but go unperceived. And suddenly someone is getting married and it is your little sister, and you are watching her look into the future with large, round, sparkling eyes; you were too busy with the mechanics of life to notice the movements of her heart, the undulations of her soul, and the explosion of her happiness.

Laila Said, Egyptian writer, *A Bridge Through Time*, 1985, p174

LIFE IS MADE
OF BLACKBERRY BUSHES
AND DARK THORNS
I WOULD HAVE LIKED IT
MORE MELLOW AND LESS BITTER …

Véronique Tadjo, poet from Côte d'Ivoire, opening lines of an untitled poem from *Latérite*, 1984 (Busby, p894)

Life is walking fast
It wasn't how I wanted it, but I had to take what I could.

Véronique Tadjo, poet from Côte d'Ivoire, opening lines of an untitled poem (Busby, p895)

The path of life is not smooth; one is bruised by its sharp edges.

Mariama Bâ, Senegalese writer, *So Long a Letter*, 1979 (1981 edition, p55)

That was life, she said to herself. Be as cunning as a serpent and as harmless as a dove.

Buchi Emecheta, Nigerian writer, *Second-Class Citizen*, 1974, chapter 2 (Partnow, *The New Quotable Woman*, p500)

... life is always much more lavish with coincidence and drama than any fiction writer dares to be.

Doris Lessing, English-Zimbabwean author, 'The Story of a Non-Marrying Man', *The Story of a Non-Marrying Man and Other Stories*, 1972 (1990 edition, p207)

Life is made up of small things, as a body is built up of cells.

Olive Schreiner, South African writer, *The Story of an African Farm*, 1883 (Penguin, 1995, p216)

Love

Don't be getting your head full of that tommy-rot. Love's for movie stars who marry four and five times and have to call it something.

Rayda Jacobs, South African author, 'The Doekoem', *Post-Cards from South Africa*, 2004, p36

I've never felt that love needed to be talked about or discussed. Love is just there. It's something you do.

Hanitra Rasoanaivo, lead singer of the Malagasy band Tarika, 'Long Way from Home', by Michal Shapiro, www.Rootsworld.com

I've always had a politicised imagination and I couldn't see politics anywhere in love. But of course,

Thank God, I grew up some and realised that you know love, like politics, is what makes the world go round and that there isn't anything that is more important than love.

Ama Ata Aidoo, Ghanaian writer (BBC World Service website)

In you I have met men
Carrying banners to the mountains
Dragging their feet upon the stones …

Shakuntala Hawoldar, Indian-born poet who married and lived in Mauritius, 'Beyond Poetry' (Chipasula & Chipasula, p139)

Love is mutually feeding each other, not one living on another like a ghoul.

Bessie Head, South African-born Botswanan writer, *A Question of Power*, 1973 (Partnow, *The Quotable Woman*, p415)

A joy and a sorrow – a help and a hindrance – love comes at last to be but what one makes it.

Pauline Smith, South African writer, 'The Schoolmaster', *The Little Karoo*, 1925 (1951 reprint, p53)

There is nothing ridiculous in love.

Olive Schreiner, South African writer, 'The Buddhist Priest's Wife', Matjiesfontein, South Africa, 1891-1892 (Clayton, p54)

I love him merely on hearing concerning him and without seeing him, and the whole story of him that hath been told me is to me as the desire of my heart, and like water to a thirsty man.

Makeda, Queen of Sheba, 10th-century BC Ethiopian queen, words before journeying to see King Solomon of Israel (Busby, p15)

Make-up and Clothing

An American woman with a coating of make-up on her face shouted at me: 'I choose to put on make-up. Why are you against the make-up? How can you call it a post-modern veil? It is a free choice! I feel I am free to do what ever I want!' I smiled and said: 'Yes, you are free like the free market, like G.W. Bush, like Ariel Sharon, like Hitler; you are free!'
Nawal El Saadawi, Egyptian writer, psychiatrist and feminist, 'Another World is Necessary', Porto Alegre, 28 January 2003

Women ... can go out dressed like drag queens en route to a gay pride march and we ... don't seem to mind. Every day, millions of women wake up, stand or sit in front of a mirror and perform a ritual of illusion and deceit that is perfectly acceptable and socially sanctioned ... Vanity and narcissism are qualities we have come to expect in women.
South African writer and journalist **Marianne Thamm**, 'It's in his hair', 29 August 2001 (*Mental Floss*, 2002, p38)

... their femininity ... was asserted once and for all by a clumsy scrawl of red across the mouth.
Doris Lessing, English-Zimbabwean author, 'Lucy Grange', *The Habit of Loving*, 1957 (*The Best of South African Short Stories*, 1991, p235)

Olive Schreiner naturally considered that too much pre-occupation with their clothes was a bad thing for the progress of women, and I have heard her call the constantly-changing female fashions 'a running sore on civilization'.

Lyndall Gregg, niece of South African writer Olive Schreiner, *Memories of Olive Schreiner*, 1957, p63

Marriage

I am looking for a man, it shall be on my terms, we will negotiate one to one …

Noerine Kaleeba, Ugandan HIV/AIDS activist, 'Noerine Kaleeba, the Brain Behind TASO', by Joe Nam, *New Vision* (Kampala), 5 April 2004

The fact that I choose to keep my name should not be defined as an act of not loving him enough.

Chika Unigwe, Nigerian writer, interview with Nnorom Azuonye, 'My E-Conversation with Chika Unigwe', *Sentinel*, March 2003

It is amazing, nay, shocking, how many perfectly independent women still view marriage as some sort of economic aid package, as if they are entering into a relationship with a bank manager with unlimited funds.

South African writer and journalist **Marianne Thamm**, 'Untying the knot', 7 November 2001 (*Mental Floss*, 2002, p55)

'No, Papa, no!' I shook my head. 'I'm not going to marry.'

I had grown into a rebel, sassy and fearless. Papa had to find me a husband while I was still a valuable commodity, because no African man wanted to be challenged by his wife. I felt sick and scared.

Waris Dirie, Somali supermodel, social activist and writer, 'The Waris Dirie Story', *Reader's Digest*, June 1999

Women ... use quite a lot of common sense: they are not particularly thrilled by the physical charms of a man; if his pockets are heavy and his income sure, he is a good matrimonial risk. But there is evolving a new type of hardheaded modern woman who insists on the perfect lover as well as an income and other necessaries, or stays forever from the unbliss of marriage.

Mabel Dove Danquah, Ghanaian writer and legislator, 'Anticipation', 1947 (Busby, p225)

Marriage, perfect marriage of mind and body is such a lovely and holy thing that rather than an imperfect travesty of it, I should say none were better.

Olive Schreiner, South African writer, letter to W T Stead (Buchanan-Gould, p146)

Martyrdom

I always wonder if I would renounce my 'cause' if I were faced with the firing squad or the hangman, especially if I got a glimpse of my young children. Would laying down my life as a sacrifice be regarded by some as selfish? Would I be satisfied to die knowing that the mere mention of my name would inspire some and forever cause some people in certain quarters to perspire?

Lola Shoneyin, Nigerian poet, interview with Nnorom Azuonye, 'My E-conversation with Lola Shoneyin', *Sentinel Poetry*, online magazine, February 2004

Once you are involved in politics, the most difficult thing is to go for hang [be sentenced to death]. That is how we look at it … So until you are killed, you can't say that you have really suffered.

Ela Ramgobin, South African anti-apartheid activist and granddaughter of Mahatma Gandhi (Russell, p133)

Materialism

Life in the consumer fast lane falls into two categories; those of us who live in the eternal hell that is Economy Class (EC), and the small but growing number of the world's elite who cruise through in Business Class (BC). Unfortunately if you fall outside of these two categories you no longer count.

South African writer and journalist **Marianne Thamm**, 'An Economy Class Life', 28 March 2001 (*Mental Floss*, 2002, p4)

'No,' she sighs, 'the more you have, the more you have to keep your head and count and check up because you know you won't notice or remember. No, if you got a lot you must keep snaps in your mind of the insides of all the cupboards. And every day, click, click, new snaps of the larder. That's why that one is so tired, always thinking, always reciting to herself the lists of what's in the cupboards. I never know what's in my cupboard at home ...

Zoë Wicomb, South African writer, 'You Can't Get Lost in Cape Town', *You Can't Get Lost in Cape Town*, 1987 (Busby, p756)

Life was far simpler than Berka supposed: If a man had children, he must provide for them. If he found society in a certain state, there was nothing he could do to change it. There had always been injustice, poverty and hardship. It was a tough materialistic world and in order to survive one had to fight it with its own weapons.

Rose Zwi, South African novelist, *Another Year in Africa*, 1980, p102

... she had seen with her own eyes some Flower Children burning money on a sidewalk to show their contempt for it; but for her part what it showed was that they must have rich parents.

Doris Lessing, English-Zimbabwean author, 'Out of the Fountain', *The Story of a Non-Marrying Man and Other Stories*, 1972 (1990 edition, p9)

What are fine clothes, and a fine skin? Well, nothing, just nothing, when you come to reason about them, and just everything when you come to look at them.

Olive Schreiner, South African writer, *Undine*, 1928 (Emslie, p140)

Media

The media sets the agenda and is the mirror through which the country looks at itself. We therefore feel that the role of the media in nation building cannot be complete without the active participation of women.

Shollo Phetlhu, acting general manager of Botswana TV (BTV), 'Women Demand Gender Equality in Batswana Media', IRIN, 13 January 2005

There is a strange culture of sycophancy sweeping though the print media. Where you have leaders who are outright failures, you'll be sure to find a journalist who will be talking as if he is the greatest thing since boob jobs. Too many journalists/writers are too happy to compromise their integrity for a few Naira.

Lola Shoneyin, Nigerian poet, interview with Nnorom Azuonye, 'My E-conversation with Lola Shoneyin', *Sentinel Poetry*, online magazine, February 2004

Are we really free to choose? … The media creates the illusion that we are free to choose but we are not free to choose. If we are injected every day, every night how beautiful you are if you are slim and with make-up, they work on the conscious and the unconscious. You think you are free but you are not … When the media works on your unconscious, this is violence. It changes your mind; it changes your behaviour. It is like a thief. It steals your intelligence from you. It's robbing you of your mind. It's sometimes more dangerous than robbing your economy or your money. With what are you going to fight?

Nawal El Saadawi, Egyptian writer, psychiatrist and feminist (www.nawalsaadawi.net)

Men

She'd lived long enough to know that you could love one man as well as another. It was all a matter of cleaning the palette between them.

Rayda Jacobs, South African author, 'Sabah', *Post-Cards from South Africa*, 2004, p195

Eno said in her days,
men were sweet and sensitive.

I spat in her divorced face
and threw the dead woman
right out of my house.

Lola Shoneyin, Nigerian poet, excerpt from 'In Eno's Days' (interview with Nnorom Azuonye, 'My E-conversation with Lola Shoneyin', *Sentinel Poetry*, online magazine, February 2004)

Men, as much as I love them, have historically cared only for themselves. Men walk away, they leave babies and all. They start wars over their stupid egos. They kill their own mothers to escape the societies who know their responsibilities.

Kola Boof, Sudanese-American writer and activist, press statement, 3 January 2003 (www.kolaboof.com)

… I like to be in their company. Although I don't necessarily want to have them under my roof.

Cesaria Evora, Cape Verdean singer, quoted in 'This Diva Kicks Off Her Shoes to Sing Cape Verde's Blues', by Don Heckman, *Los Angeles Times*, 7 October 1995

I knew that in order to be considered the equal of a man in that milieu [parliament], I had to be better than them, and that it wasn't too difficult because, really, most of them were third-rate.

Helen Suzman, South African parliamentarian, 1995 interview, *Cutting Through the Mountain*, p440

'Boys always fight for things that are not theirs.' From her own experience, the word *boys* could be substituted by *men*. Yes, men, or at least some of them, always fight for things that are not theirs.

Ifeoma Okoye, Nigerian writer, 'The Pay-packet' (Bruner, *African Women's Writing*, p16)

Men were the first gods in the universe, and they were devouring gods.

Ama Ata Aidoo, Ghanaian writer, *Changes: A Love Story*, 1991, p110

None of you [men] ask for anything – except everything, but just for so long as you need it.

Doris Lessing, English-Zimbabwean author, *The Golden Notebook*, 1962, *Free Women*, 5 (Kaplan, p746)

Some men are fat, and some men are thin; some men drink brandy and some men drink gin; but it all comes to the same thing in the end; it's all one. A man's a man, you know.

Olive Schreiner, South African writer, *The Story of an African Farm*, 1883 (Penguin, 1995, p293)

Modelling

When someone suggested I become a model I thought they were mad. I could see what magazines were looking for in the early 1970s. It was blonde, blue-eyed Aryan girls, not black ones. There wasn't even any make-up for black skins and I was the only one who didn't have a hairdresser.

Esther Kamatari, Burundian princess and former fashion model, 'Cat-walk Princess Seeks Power in Burundi', by Kim Willsher, 7 November 2004 (www.telegraph.co.uk/news)

Models are an alien life form – they come from the planet Perfecto. Twenty years ago models weighed on average eight per cent less than the average woman. Today it's 25 per cent.

Pnina Fenster, South African magazine editor, 'Glam Ed Pnina Joins Glossy Possy', by Gillian McAinsh, *LA Femme*, 10 January 2004

It was fun, but it was meaningless.

> On modelling, **Waris Dirie**, Somali supermodel, social activist and writer, 'Somalia's Desert Flower', by Helen Gibson, *Time Europe* magazine, 15 July 2002

Money

Money is the crack, Father! Don't you see? History is just money blazing its trail across the earth, even if there are a thousand different variations of it. Our own history is nothing but a trail of greed.

> **Dalene Matthee**, South African novelist, *The Day the Swallows Spoke*, 1992, p116

In any language, BMW remain the three most prominent letters in our vocabulary.

> **Carolyn Sacks**, South African journalist (Crwys-Williams, p217)

Money is a difficult thing to keep, especially when it is scarce.

> Words of the character Mr Matimba, in **Tsitsi Dangarembga**, Zimbabwean writer, *Nervous Conditions*, 1988, p29

'I used to feed myself for ten shillings a week!'
'But why? What for? What's the point?'
'Because I was free, that's the point! If you don't spend a lot of money, then you don't have to earn and you are free.'

> **Doris Lessing**, English-Zimbabwean author, 'The Story of a Non-Marrying Man', *The Story of a Non-Marrying Man and Other Stories*, 1972 (1990 edition, p210)

Mortality

Our huts and the old mulberry tree and the little
brown mat of earth that my mother dug over
yesterday, way down there, and way over there the
clump of trees round the chimneys and the shiny
thing that is the TV mast of the farmhouse – they
are nothing, on the back of this earth. It could
twitch them away like a dog does a fly.

> **Nadine Gordimer**, South African writer, 'Amnesty', *Jump and
> Other Stories*, 1991, p256

Those stars that shone on up above so quietly,
they had seen a thousand such little existences, a
thousand such little existences fight so fiercely, flare
up just so brightly, and go out; and they, the old, old
stars shone on for ever.

> **Olive Schreiner**, South African writer, *The Story of an African
> Farm*, 1883 (Penguin, 1995, p120)

There is a strange coming and going of feet. Men
appear, act and re-act upon each other and pass
away, when the crisis comes the man who would
fit it does not return, when the curtain falls no one
is ready. When the footlights are brightest they are
blown out ...

> **Olive Schreiner**, South African writer, *The Story of An African
> Farm*, preface, 1883 (Buchanan-Gould, p65)

Motherhood

I am so sorry ma
that I am not
what I so much want to be for you

Antjie Krog, South African poet and writer, *A Change of
Tongue*, 2003, p110

We are all mothers,
and we have that fire within us,
…
What terrible thing can you do to us
which we have not done to ourselves?

Abena P A Busia, Ghanaian poet, 'Liberation', 1983 (Chipasula
& Chipasula, p53)

Life never comes unaccompanied to a woman, death
is always right behind, furtive, quick, and smiling at
the mothers.

Assia Djebar, Algerian novelist, 'There Is No Exile', *Women in
Their Apartments*, 1980 (www.kirjasto.sci.fi)

Mother, I need you. Though a woman grown,
Mine own self's arbitrator, mine own law,
My need of you is deeper than I've known …

Gladys May Casely-Hayford, Ghanaian-Sierra Leonean poet,
first lines of 'To My Mother' (Busby, p219)

A mother's responsibility is never over, that's what
I say. When they're little, it's little troubles; when
they're grown up, it's big ones.

Nadine Gordimer, South African writer, 'Enemies', *Six Feet of the Country*, 1956 (*The Best of South African Short Stories*, 1991, p220)

We bear the world, and *we* make it. The souls of little children are marvellously delicate and tender things, and keep for ever the shadow that first falls on them, and that is the mother's or at best a woman's. There was never a great man who had not a great mother – it is hardly an exaggeration.

Olive Schreiner, South African writer, *The Story of an African Farm*, 1883 (Penguin, 1995, p193)

Music

Song is the province of women. Women sing lullabies, songs of marriage, songs that describe the difficulty of life, and songs that celebrate the happiness of love.

'20 Ans Barakat' [20 Years is Enough], Algerian women's group (www.globalfundforwomen.org)

Sometimes a song is worth a thousand speeches.

'20 Ans Barakat' [20 Years is Enough], Algerian women's group (www.globalfundforwomen.org)

Music is really the thread of the memory of humankind.

Angélique Kidjo, Beninois musician (www.giantstep.net)

Faith made me sing.

Nahawa Doumbia, Malian singer, interview with Kristell Diallo, March 2001, New York (Afropop Worldwide)

A lot of women sing love songs, but I'm a fighter. I fight for children's education and for marriage – particularly for monogamy. Good relationships are very important. You have to work in order to succeed.

Nahawa Doumbia, Malian singer, 'Mali Singer Nahawa Doumbia Opens Young Ears', by Chris Nickson, 22 May 2000, VH1.com

Music is not like war. Music is another way.

Ramata Diakité, Malian singer, speaking in 1999 (Afropop Worldwide website, contribution by Banning Eyre)

Music is not just a commodity you just buy and sell. It is pure, clean, and … to me, even sacred. It fulfills the emotional senses. Music is about passion. It is life enhancing, even intoxicating … I respect it because I believe it is a God-given gift …

Ethiopian singer **Aster Aweke**, interview in *Ethiopian Review*, July 1997 (ethiopianreview.homestead.com)

The morna is really a way of expressing love, sadness, leaving our families behind. All Cape Verdeans at one point have to sing a morna to express our feelings.

Cesaria Evora, Cape Verdean singer describing a distinctive national style of music called *mornas* (Yawu Miller, 'Cape Verdean Singer Brings Island "Mornas" to World Stage', *Bay State Banner*, 14 November 1996)

Nature and Animals

You who're so clever ought to know that proteas belong to the veld. Only fools and cowards would hand them over to the Boers. Those who put their stamp on things may see in it their own histories and hopes. But a bush is a bush; it doesn't become what people think they inject into it.

> **Zoë Wicomb**, South African writer, 'A Trip to the Gifberge', 1987 (Medalie, p133)

This is a calm sea, generally. Too calm in fact, this Gulf of Guinea. The natives sacrifice to him on Tuesdays and once a year celebrate him ... he doesn't pay much attention to it either.

> **Ama Ata Aidoo**, Ghanaian writer, 'Two Sisters', *No Sweetness Here*, 1970 (1995 edition, pp95-96)

Does it ever strike you as such a comfort that wherever you wander there will always be solid earth and sky, something of nature near you, even if it be obscured by house and smoke.

> **Olive Schreiner**, South African writer, letter to Karl Pearson, 18 February 1886 (Beeton, p100)

Nigeria

I fervently believe in the Nigerian project ... there is the wonderful women factor; great dishes; funny political realities; strong religious culture; access to self education and actualization and then, everyone born into this country becomes a bread winner, with no age restrictions; moreover there is this economy of ours that in spite of murderous policies has refused to die.

Remi Adedeji, Nigerian writer, 'I Love Nigeria, I No Go Lie', *The Sun News* online, 7 March 2004

When as a writer you get a bad reaction from the Nigerian government, you are obviously doing something right.

Lola Shoneyin, Nigerian poet, interview with Nnorom Azuonye, 'My E-conversation with Lola Shoneyin', *Sentinel Poetry*, online magazine, February 2004

My whole family lives in America, but I am passionate about this place because I see the potential. And the potential is not just in the oil and gas, it's in human beings.

Christine Anyanwu, Nigerian journalist (interview on website Frontline World)

If one claims to believe in Nigeria, and in the unity in diversity idea, then one must embrace the study and investigation of Biafra because Nigeria would not be today as it is if Biafra had not been.

Chimamanda Ngozi Adichie, Nigerian novelist, 'In the Footsteps of Chinua Achebe: Enter Chimamanda Ngozi Adichie, Nigeria's Newest Literary Voice', by Ike Anya, *Sentinel Poetry*, online magazine, November 2003

The news that Aduka had ... become a public woman spread throughout Lagos like wildfire. Ibuza men gloried in the unfaithfulness of women: 'Leave them for ten minutes, they turn into something else.' Many people put the blame on Lagos itself; they said it was a fast town which could corrupt the most innocent of girls.

Buchi Emecheta, Nigerian writer, *The Joys of Motherhood*, 1979, p170

They say Lagos men do not just chase women, they snatch them.

Flora Nwapa, Nigerian novelist, *This is Lagos*, 1971 (Bruner, *Unwinding Threads*, p40)

Night

There was no sky as totally black as an African sky, where the stars hung so low that one could almost reach out to pluck them from the heavens.

Farida Karodia, South African-Canadian writer, *A Shattering of Silence*, 1993, p216

Just before light, when it's supposed to be darkest, the body's at its lowest ebb and in the hospital on the hill old people die – the night opens, a Black Hole between stars, and from it comes a deep panting.

Nadine Gordimer, South African writer, 'A Lion on the Freeway', *A Soldier's Embrace*, 1975 (1983 edition, p24)

The great dome of the sky was heavy with its
blazing constellations, lesser stars powdered the
Milky Way and the spread-eagled Southern Cross
dreamed in the hammock of the night. It could fall,
thought Roxane, I could catch it in my hands ...

Joy Packer, South African novelist, *Valley of the Vines*, 1955, p85

There is no twilight in East Africa. Night tramps on
the heels of Day with little gallantry and takes the
place she lately held, in severe and humourless
silence.

Beryl Markham, English-born East African aviator, *West With
the Night*, 1942 (Penguin 1988 edition, p39)

Oppression

The physical is visible, and sometimes the visible is
less dangerous than the invisible oppression.

Nawal El Saadawi, Egyptian writer, psychiatrist and feminist,
quoted in 'Nawal el Saadawi – A Creative and Dissident Life',
by Brian Belton and Clare Dowding (www.infed.org)

... I have been losing
myself in the smell of the kitchen steam

Shakuntala Hawoldar, Mauritian poet, 'You Have Touched My
Skin' (Chipasula & Chipasula, p137)

Since she is my sister's child
Atieno needs no pay ...

Marjorie Oludhe Macgoye, Kenyan poet, 'A Freedom Song'
(Chipasula & Chipasula, p120)

Freedom is not defined only in terms of colour. If it is wrong for whites to oppress blacks, then it is even more immoral and shameful for black African leaders to oppress their own people.

Makaziwe Mandela, South African academic, February 1992 (Ayittey, p xi)

Born to suffer
When shall Nkosi Sikelel'iAfrika? ...

Because of my colour and my sex
When shall Nkosi Sikelela me?

Excerpts from the poem 'One Woman's History' by South African activist **R Machaba** (Barbara Schreiner, p64)

Her mother, brother and sister were in cells, somewhere. All the time. While they ate, while they worked, while they took the dog for his walk. For that progression of repetitions known as daily life went on; with only a realization of how strange it is, in its dogged persistence.

Nadine Gordimer, South African author, 'Home', *Jump and Other Stories*, 1991, p131

Optimism

It's not where you come from, but where you are going that matters.

Felicia Mabuza-Suttle, South African talkshow host (*Great South Africans*, 2004, p192)

... all jailhouses open on a garden.
Calixthe Beyala, Cameroonian novelist, *Maman a un amant*,
1993 (iupjournals.org)

And I believe in the power of art and in living in
harmony with the environment and in the possi-
bility of a good society.
Ann Cluver Weinberg, South African writer and music
teacher, 'The B Minor Mass – South Africa 1986', 1986 (Carr,
p129)

Parenthood

Parents, I tell you. They put you out in this dinghy
without a life jacket, then blame you if you drown.
Rayda Jacobs, South African author, 'I Count the Bullets
Sometimes', *Post-Cards from South Africa*, 2004, p58

... we Africans are taught that anyone older than
you is a parent ...
Ruth Mompati, South African anti-apartheid activist (Russell,
p109)

It's a sad moment, really, when parents first become
a bit frightened of their children.
Ama Ata Aidoo, Ghanaian writer, *Fragment from a Lost Diary
and Other Stories*, Naomi Katz and Nancy Milton (eds), 1973
(Partnow, *The Quotable Woman*, p459)

Passion

... the heart has a way of going in its own way
without listening to the head ...

Ama Ata Aidoo, Ghanaian writer (BBC World Service website)

And what a miracle it was to me, being able to say,
not: That is an attractive man, I want him, I shall
have him, but: My house is on fire, that was the
man, yes, it was he again, there he was, he has set
light to my soul.

Doris Lessing, English-Zimbabwean author, 'An Unposted
Love Letter', *The Story of a Non-Marrying Man and Other
Stories*, 1972 (1990 edition, p32)

... maybe marriage and that other love were not to
be confused. Maybe the marriages that lasted were
built on trust and not on passion.

Joy Packer, South African novelist, *Valley of the Vines*, 1955,
p155

There is a love that begins in the head, and goes
down to the heart, and grows slowly; but it lasts till
death, and asks less than it gives. There is another
love, that blots out wisdom, that is sweet with the
sweetness of life and bitter with the bitterness of
death, lasting for an hour; but it is worth having
lived a whole life for that hour.

Olive Schreiner, South African writer, *The Story of an African
Farm*, 1883 (Penguin, 1995, p228)

Past (The)

A memory marks us more than the act itself. The act is not what's important, it's the remaining trace of the event that is. No one has the same way of perceiving an act, we can all be witnesses of an explosion but we will all have seen something different.

Werewere Liking, Cameroonian playwright, interview with Michelle Mielly, Ki-Yi Village, Abidjan, Côte d'Ivoire, 2 June 2002 (African Postcolonial Literature in the Postcolonial Web)

That is the beauty of the past; there it lies on the table: journals, pictures, a candle-glass, a few books of history. You leave it and come back to it and it waits for you – unchanged. You can turn back the pages, look again at the beginning. You can leaf forward and know the end. And you tell the story that they, the people who lived it, could only tell in part.

Ahdaf Soueif, Egyptian novelist, *The Map of Love*, 1999 (www.amazon.com)

There are those who forget or who simply sleep. And then there are those who keep bumping into the walls of the past. May God take pity on them!

Assia Djebar, Algerian novelist, 'There Is No Exile', *Women in Their Apartments*, 1980 (www.kirjasto.sci.fi)

Peace

Recognizing that sustainable development, democracy and peace are indivisible is an idea whose time has come.

Wangari Maathai, Kenyan environmental and human rights activist, Nobel Lecture after receiving the Nobel Peace Prize, Oslo, Norway, 10 December 2004

They ... turned away from peace and adopted the machete.

Esther Kamatari, Burundian princess and former fashion model, 'Cat-walk Princess Seeks Power in Burundi', by Kim Willsher, 7 November 2004 (www.telegraph.co.uk/news)

I should like to see my children happy. And the happiness of my children is to have the world in peace.

Lina Magaia, Mozambican writer, 'My Century', *BBC World Service*, 16 December 1999

On all sides we must creep out of our wretched little trenches of national hatred and antagonism, dug for us by ignorance and the desire for vulgar dominance and empire ... and we must meet on the same ground of common humanity; each bearing in his hand something he is willing to give up, and the strongest and the greatest giving most.

Olive Schreiner, South African writer, letter to a Peace Meeting in London, held under the auspices of the Union of Democratic Control, during the First World War (Buchanan-Gould, p235)

The Governments have made the wars – the peoples themselves must make the peace!

Olive Schreiner, South African writer, speech on behalf of the Union of Democratic Control, 11 March 1916 (www.spartacus. schoolnet.co.uk)

Permanence

You see these cycles in a life, and then you see them in nations … You see when you think of what I have seen go – first the good old British empire which disappeared when it was supposed to last for ever; Hitler was ranting and raving about a thousand years' rule; Mussolini; the Soviet Union seemed indestructible; the white dominated societies of Southern Africa seemed everlasting … I would have found it impossible to believe that the one in southern Rhodesia could go just like that. All these things have gone as if they never were, so you don't have, at my age, much of a belief in permanence.

Doris Lessing, English-Zimbabwean author (BBC World Service website)

There are two things that never change – the Pyramids and the voice of Om Kulthum.

Egyptian saying; Om Kulthum was the most revered Egyptian songstress of the 20th century (www.iearnegypt. org)

Poetry

A poem must be before it can mean.
> **Toyin Adewale-Gabriel**, Nigerian writer, 'My E-Conversation with Toyin Adewale-Gabriel', by Nnorom Azuonye, *Sentinel Poetry*, online magazine, November 2003

The more I think about it, the less I can imagine an enemy of poetry. Poetry will continue long after you and I are gone, long after civilizations of which we were once part have been brought to nothing.
> **Antjie Krog**, South African poet and writer (*Great South Africans*, 2004, p202)

In our region poets can go to prison ... A piece of poetry can make a revolution.
> **Nawal El Saadawi**, Egyptian writer, psychiatrist and feminist, 'Conversation with Dr Nawal el Saadawi', interview by Stephanie McMillan, 1999

Politicians

It's sickening how it's used for political ends. These people are just pawns for politicians like Jeb Bush.
> On the death penalty, **Charlize Theron**, South African actress, 'Out of Africa', Emma Brockes, *The Guardian*, 2 April 2004 (http://film.guardian.co.uk)

The South African politician, although elected by the people, for the people, is seldom actually seen moving among the people.

From *The How-to-Be a South African Handbook*, by South
African writers **Marianne Thamm** and Toby Newsome, 2002,
p6

... more and more African states resemble a crumbling house from which both the owner and the onlookers scramble to escape with whatever can be looted. As a result, the civil society mistrusts and dislikes politicians and civil servants perceiving them as self-serving, greedy and corrupt.

Wangari Maathai, Kenyan environmental and human rights
activist, 'Bottle-Necks of Development in Africa', paper
presented at the 4th UN World Women's Conference in
Beijing, China, August-September 1995

Politics

Although politics has given me a rough life, there is absolutely nothing I regret about what I have done and what has happened to me and my family throughout all these years. Instead, I have been strengthened and feel more of a woman than I would otherwise.

Albertina Sisulu, South African nurse, liberation leader, and
wife of Walter Sisulu (*Great South Africans*, 2004, p166)

Women's involvement in political life is part of their significant roles in society. They have to participate in political life, to proceed to vote, to submit their candidature in parliamentary councils, to interact with the society, and give opinions and thoughts to achieve their goals in society not to be dependent on men.

> **Dr Fawzeya Abdelsattar Aly**, Egyptian politician and law professor (www.iearnegypt.org)

African women need to overcome social, cultural and traditional barriers before they can be accepted on the political scene.

> **Agathe Uwilingiyimana**, Rwandan prime minister, Kenya's *Daily Nation*, 9 March 1996, p18

Politics has nothing to do with growing a beard on your face, but has everything to do with standing on your own two feet.

> **Nana Rawlings**, first lady of Ghana, comment made at a luncheon in Washington, DC, *Africa Today*, January-February 1996, p37

In South Africa you don't decide to join politics; politics decides to join you.

> **Ruth Mompati**, South African anti-apartheid activist (Russell, p91)

Last night the white women convicts tapped on the lavatory wall to ask why I was being kept locked up all the time.

'I'm in for theft, what are you in for?'

'Sedition.'

'What's that?'

'Politics.'

'Is that all – man, they're bloody mad!'

Amy Reitstein, South African activist, 'Sedition – Is That All?'
(Barbara Schreiner, p74)

Poverty

The three richest people in the world have more
assets than the three least developed countries
combined. That is totally unacceptable.
> **Nkosazana Dlamini-Zuma**, South African Minister of Foreign
> Affairs (*Great South Africans*, 2004, p208)

Everywhere there are smells of smoked fish, beer,
peanuts and dead rats, all mixed together, churned
up in nausea. I am strolling along, meditating over
these emanations of grub and filth.
> **Calixthe Beyala**, Cameroonian novelist, *Your Name Shall Be
> Tanga* [*Tu t'appelleras Tanga*], 1988 (iupjournals.org)

Do you think a poor country like this shouldn't have
the right to something that grand?
> **Local woman** questioning a Westerner about the oft-
> criticised Basilica of Our Lady of Peace, a grandiose structure
> in Yamoussoukro, Houphouët-Boigny's home village; quoted
> by Lance Morrow, 'Africa: The Scramble for Existence', *Time*, 7
> September 1992

Perhaps I like food so much because I've been poor
... But there are deeper causes for human suffering
and starvation – perhaps found in the realm of the
spirit.

Bessie Head, South African-born Botswanan writer, *The Best of South African Short Stories*, 1991, p323

It seemed incredible that in the midst of such squalor, conditions so purgatorial, antipathetic to life, people could be fine. At least at Middledrift and at Tsolo everything was on their side – the peace, the grandeurs of the scene, the environment to which they could feel they belonged. Did not those settings enable people to share their life's sacraments and pleasures? And what in heaven's name, in these other surroundings could prompt the spirit?

Noni Jabavu, South African writer, *The Ochre People: Scenes from a South African Life*, 1963, chapter XVI (Busby, p293)

Power

Women are owners of the wombs. They are life. If women got together and screamed, the earth will shake. Such is the power that we wield. We should use that power and shout down the war.

Chika Unigwe, Nigerian writer, interview with Nnorom Azuonye, 'My E-Conversation with Chika Unigwe', *Sentinel*, March 2003

Power with no responsibility is a political disease inherited with the class patriarchal system born with slavery. It is one of the dichotomies forced on us by religion and philosophy. We have to undo this split between good divine power and the Devil's

responsibility for evil. We have to un-mask the
language of G W Bush the father, the son, and the
holy ghost and his axis of evil.

Nawal El Saadawi, Egyptian writer, psychiatrist and feminist,
'Another World is Necessary', Porto Alegre, 28 January 2003

The measure of its women is ultimately the measure
of any people's strength and resistile power.

Olive Schreiner, South African writer, *Thoughts on South
Africa*, 1923 (1992 edition, p21)

Pregnancy and Childbirth

Sister, you cannot think a baby out!

Title of a poem by **Irène Assiba d'Almeida**, Beninois poet
(Chipasula & Chipasula, p41)

… Every birth
new eyes squinting in pain at a new world.

Marjorie Oludhe Macgoye, Kenyan poet, 'August the First:
Court Martial. The Mother Speaks' (Maja-Pearce, p16)

'Do you know what they call pregnancy in
Afrikaans?'
　　'No.' Her tone was expectant, interested.
　　'*Die ander tyd*' ['The other time'].
　　'Good heavens – but that's very accurate.'

Cherry Clayton, South African writer, 'In Time's Corridor'
(*The Best of South African Short Stories*, 1991, p286)

The mere labour of child-bearing in itself, under whatever conditions performed, will not always prove beneficial to society.

Olive Schreiner, South African writer (Buchanan-Gould, p225)

Presidential Candidacy

I am not down and out. Those writing me off are doing so at their own peril.

Charity Ngilu, Kenyan politician, 'Ngilu: Don't Write Me Off Yet', interview with Bob Odalo, 6 February 2005, *The Nation*, Nairobi

I don't want power, I want to change things. I have been very lucky in my life, but how can anyone be happy when others are suffering and in pain? And the people of Burundi are in pain.

Esther Kamatari, Burundian princess and former fashion model, on why she is running for president, 'Cat-walk Princess Seeks Power in Burundi', by Kim Willsher, 7 November 2004 (www.telegraph.co.uk/news)

Men have been dominating Malawi politics for too long. Maybe that's why they are blundering. But I think that if a woman can come up, she would improve a lot of things.

Vera Chirwa, Malawian lawyer and human rights activist, 'Malawi Activist to Run for Office', by Grant Ferrett, *BBC News*, 4 January 2004

It's time for women to rise up, it's time for Benin to come out of its underdeveloped shell, and finally, it's time for Marie-Elise Akouavi Gbedo to become president.

Marie-Elise Akouavi Gbedo, Beninois lawyer and first female presidential candidate, explaining her campaign slogan 'Huenusu' meaning 'It's time' in the Fon language, 'First Female Presidential Candidate in Benin', 22 February 2001, by Michee Boko, IPS (www.afrol.com)

Progress

The only way forward was to go slowly and be totally prepared for the worst.

Maganthrie Pillay, South African filmmaker, 'Creating, Above All Else', by Nils van der Linden, 13 January 2005 (iafrica.com)

Apprenticeship to traditional crafts seems degrading to whoever has the slightest book-learning. The dream is to become a clerk. The trowel is spurned ...

Should we have been happy at the desertion of the forges, the workshops, the shoemaker's shops? Should we have rejoiced so wholeheartedly? Were we not beginning to witness the disappearance of an elite of traditional manual workers?

Eternal questions of our eternal debates. We all agreed that much dismantling was needed to introduce modernity within our traditions. Torn between the past and the present, we deplored the 'hard sweat' that would be inevitable. We counted the possible losses. But we knew that nothing would be as before. We were full of nostalgia but were resolutely progressive.

> **Mariama Bâ**, Senegalese writer, *Une Si longue letter (So Long A Letter)*, 1979, chapter 8 (Busby, pp342-43)

Here we stand
infants overblown,
poised between two civilizations,
finding the balance irksome ....

> **Mabel Imoukhuede**, Nigerian poet (Bryan, p13)

The old must always make room for the young, and if we do it ungrudgingly so much the better for ourselves.

> **Elsa Smithers**, South African farmer, *March Hare*, 1935, p212

A train is better than an ox-wagon only when it carries better men; rapid movement is an advantage only when we move towards beauty and truth; all motion is not advance, all change is not development ...

> **Olive Schreiner**, South African writer, *Thoughts on South Africa*, 1923 (1976 Africana Book Society reprint, p329)

Racism and Prejudice

Blacks and whites were not really friends in South Africa – we English have a history of arrogance and a stubborn refusal to accept, understand and forgive others.

> **Ginn Fourie**, South African professor, whose daughter Lyndi was killed by anti-apartheid soldiers in the Heidelberg Tavern

attack in Cape Town in 1993, article in *Huisgenoot* & *You* magazines, 2003

People ask me 'how can you marry such a white man?' I say 'he's just a man. I don't see any color.' Do you think it would be better if we all looked the same? Just one color everywhere would be so boring.'

Angélique Kidjo, Beninois musician, 'Angélique Kidjo: Solving the Crossover Problem', by Mike Zwerin, 4 May 2001 (Kulturekiosque website)

My grandmother, my grandfather, my aunts and uncles all told me the story when I was small and I was really scared. If you are bad the Senegalese will come and eat you. It was the classic colonial divide-and-rule tactic. If it is blacker than you, it is nasty and inhuman and does these terrible things.

Hanitra Rasoanaivo, singer with the Malagasy band Tarika, speaking about their album *Tarika: Son Egal*, on which they are joined by Senegalese musicians ('African War and Peace', by Nigel Williamson, *Times* newspapers, 1997)

And if the white man thought that Asians were a low, filthy nation, Asians could still smile with relief – at least, they were not Africans. And if the white man thought that Africans were a low, filthy nation, Africans in southern Africa could still smile – at least, they were not bushmen. They all have their monsters.

Bessie Head, South African-born Botswanan writer, *Maru*, Pt I, 1971 (Partnow, *The Quotable Woman*, p415)

Is there really any superiority at all implied in degrees of pigmentation, and are the European races, except in their egoistic distortion of imagination, more desirable or highly developed than the Asiatic?

Olive Schreiner, South African writer, *From Man to Man*, 1927 (Emslie, p520)

Rebellion

Wouldn't it be nice to be a lady of leisure? I'd have to learn to be a lady first.

Diane Awerbuck, South African writer, 'It's Not About the Therapy', by Nils van der Linden, 27 January 2005 (iafrica. com)

Quietly, unobtrusively and extremely fitfully, something in my mind began to assert itself, to question things and refuse to be brainwashed, bringing me to this time when I can set down this story. It was a long and painful process for me, that process of expansion. It was a process whose events stretched over many years and would fill another volume ...

Tsitsi Dangarembga, Zimbabwean writer, *Nervous Conditions*, 1988

I cannot obey any boss without questioning, be he the head of state.

Nawal El Saadawi, Egyptian writer, psychiatrist and feminist, 'Exile and Resistance', Cairo, November 2002

I always wanted to know the reasons for things and didn't like when I was smacked for asking or pushed away or ignored. So I became my own person. I was considered different. Inside I felt I was right.

Waris Dirie, Somali supermodel, social activist and writer, 'Somalia's Desert Flower', by Helen Gibson, *Time Europe* magazine, 15 July 2002

'And what lessons does this teach us, my dear?'

'That God has prepared a heaven for the people he means to save and a hell for the people he means to burn,' said Undine, very gravely, never raising her eyes from the carpet on which they rested …

'I would much sooner be wicked and go to hell than be good only because I was afraid of going there,' said Undine …

Olive Schreiner, South African writer, *Undine*, 1928 (Emslie, p12)

Reconciliation

I see a bright future for our country if we can get together and blend the best of our cultures. Instead of honing our weapons for war, we could beat them into ploughshares. The politicians aren't going to do it for us. We ordinary South Africans are going to have to do it.

Ginn Fourie, South African professor, whose daughter Lyndi was killed by anti-apartheid soldiers in the Heidelberg Tavern attack in Cape Town in 1993, article in *Huisgenoot* & *You* magazines, 2003

When people have been belittled and humiliated for as long as they have been in South Africa, violence becomes inevitable. If you know how people have been hurt, you can start breaking the cycle, for future generations.

Ginn Fourie, South African professor, whose daughter Lyndi was killed by anti-apartheid soldiers in the Heidelberg Tavern attack in Cape Town in 1993, article in *Huisgenoot* & *You* magazines, 2003

Come, let us collect wood and build a fire. We will burn our old lives, turn the clocks back until they tell the right time for us ...

Sheila Fugard, South African novelist and poet, *The Castaways*, 1972 (2002 edition, p72)

Refugees

So they decided – our grandmother did; our grandfather made little noises and rocked from side to side, but she took no notice – we would go away. We children were pleased. We wanted to go away from where our mother wasn't and where we were hungry. We wanted to go where there were no bandits and there was food. We were glad to think there must be such a place; away.

Nadine Gordimer, South African writer, 'The Ultimate Safari', *Telling Tales*, 2004, p271

We have no where to go. It is not easy to live in another man's country but your own.

Ruth Perry, Former Interim Head of State of Liberia, speaking at ECOWAS-led peace talks in August 2003 in Ghana ('We Wonna Go Home! – The Liberian Story', by Nana Kodjo Jehu-Appiah, 29 August 2003, GNA)

Rejection

'… all I want to know is, did he love me or didn't he love me?'

'If you even have to ask that question, Araminta, the answer is no.'

Dalene Matthee, South African novelist, *The Day the Swallows Spoke*, 1992, p17

We cannot help love's going, any more than we can help its coming; and when it is gone, it is better to say so.

Olive Schreiner, South African writer, in a letter to friend Erilda Cawood, 1879 (Fogg, p13)

She thought her heart was broken. Perhaps it was; but she did not know that hearts are only Time's china cups – china cups which the old father is forever throwing hither and thither, cracking and smashing in his wild reckless way, and then carefully picking up and cementing so cleverly that the old scar does not even show. They may ring a little dead if you strike them – but that is all.

Olive Schreiner, South African writer, *Undine*, 1928 (Emslie, p42)

Religion

My religion is called THE WOMB, because I believe
that only through a conscious women's religious
movement can the world be healed, delivered from
poverty and oppression, and most of all, delivered
from the inhumane and psychotic evils of the
current man-made religions that are a plague
against my children.

> **Kola Boof**, Sudanese-American writer and activist, press
> statement, 3 January 2003 (www.kolaboof.com)

I am fascinated by the power of religion. I grew up
Catholic, still am, although I am what may be called
a Liberal Catholic, which is that I believe in Lourdes
but also think that contraception is a good thing.

> **Chimamanda Ngozi Adichie**, Nigerian novelist, 'In the
> Footsteps of Chinua Achebe: Enter Chimamanda Ngozi
> Adichie, Nigeria's Newest Literary Voice', by Ike Anya, *Sentinel
> Poetry*, online magazine, November 2003

I think that holy men hear an awful lot of bullshit in
the line of duty.

> **Diane Awerbuck**, South African writer, *Gardening at Night*,
> 2003, p4

Voodoo has a bad reputation. Why? Because the
colonialists found that the voodoo religion brings
our people together. They didn't want that.

> **Angélique Kidjo**, Beninois musician, 'Angélique Kidjo:
> Solving the Crossover Problem', by Mike Zwerin, 4 May 2001
> (Kulturekiosque website)

The religious ritual and creed may or may not be rejected later in life but the moral code can provide a sturdy ethical foundation.

Helena Dolny, agricultural economist and second wife of South African politician Joe Slovo, writing in 1995, *Cutting Through the Mountain*, p223

When people are on the the point of death they often (re)turn to religion but Joe firmly stated that he wanted a secular funeral and to be buried in a secular graveyard; he did not want relatives to claim for him in death that which he had chosen to relinquish in life.

Helena Dolny, agricultural economist and second wife of South African politician Joe Slovo, writing in 1995, *Cutting Through the Mountain*, p243

If I was to meet those slave raiders that abducted me and those who tortured me, I'd kneel down to them to kiss their hands, because, if it had not have been for them, I would not have become a Christian and religious woman.

Josephine Bakhita, Sudanese Catholic saint (afrol News)

'Religion is like love,' answered Undine. 'It flourishes best in silence, and is to be felt, not spoken of.'

Olive Schreiner, South African writer, *Undine*, 1928 (Emslie, p55)

Religious Fundamentalism

For us, religious fundamentalism is a form of terror-ism against women. Its manifestations are varied but its purpose is the same everywhere: the control of women and therefore the refusal to recognise them as autonomous human beings and as citizens.

Louisa Ait-Hamou, Algerian activist, 'Women's Struggle Against Muslim Fundamentalism in Algeria: Strategies or a Lesson For Survival?' (www.whrnet.org)

I don't believe in anyone who tells me, 'You've got to kill yourself in the name of God.' Every time you take a life, you're taking God's life.

Angélique Kidjo, Beninois musician (www.giantstep.net)

Algerian women writers live under the twin threats of religious fundamentalism and a quasi-fascist military regime. For us, women's issues are issues of survival, our financial resources are nil and our psychological balance is weakened by fear and anxiety ... The intimidations of the regime and the threats of the Islamists have one purpose: to reduce us to silence. Fear is supposed to drive us away from critical thinking and writing, or stress and exile render us unable to produce any literary creation ... Arab and Muslim women need not only to have their lives saved, but also opportunities to create and write. Our voices must be strengthened ...

Acha Lemsine, Algerian author, 1995 essay ('Algeria's Civil War Takes Toll on Female Journalists', web article for International Pen Women's Day, 8 March 2003)

Repatriation

'Why do you want to come back, Sabah?'
  'For the smell of the sea.'
  'That's it?'
  'I left my soul at the foot of Table Mountain. I want it back.'

Rayda Jacobs, South African author, 'For the Smell of the Sea', *Post-Cards from South Africa*, 2004, p100

The word 'strange' or 'stranger' began to hunt me down wherever I went in my own country at first then later when I travelled abroad. Abroad it changed to become the English word 'alien'. When I hear the word 'alien' I put my hands over my ears to shut it out, for it is a very painful word, a word which deprives me of my human rights and dignity. It forces me to take the plane back to my country, for exile in one's home is less cruel than exile in a foreign country.

Nawal El Saadawi, Egyptian writer, psychiatrist and feminist, 'Exile and Resistance', Cairo, November 2002

In Somali we have a word, *nurro*, it means instinct. Animals, and those who escape death, have the gift of *nurro* from Allah. It is how the termites build a home out of their own saliva, it's how a lizard knows to break out of its egg and find something to eat. I wanted to believe in my *nurro*, but I worried that I had been away too long. I didn't know how to read the signs anymore.

Waris Dirie, Somali supermodel, social activist and writer, *Desert Dawn*, 2002 (www.virago.co.uk)

She had thought about going back. Her grandmother had strongly advised her to do so. No. She could not. To have to adapt herself again, to start all over from the beginning ... As if such a thing were possible. Go back for what? To vegetate behind the blinds of a city going nowhere and peer out at the women bringing water from Madeiral in cans on their heads or the men dragging carts loaded with sacks to the Morais warehouse?

No, no, forever, no.

Orlanda Amarílis, Cape Verdean writer, 'Disillusion' (Bruner, *African Women's Writing*, p35)

Resistance

No Iran, No Sudan, Algeria is Algerian.

Slogan of **Algerian women's movement** (found in Louisa Ait-Hamou's paper 'Women's Struggle Against Muslim Fundamentalism in Algeria: Strategies or a Lesson For Survival?' on www.whrnet.org)

If you are unable to resist and fight nationally, then try to resist and fight internationally, so you can function ... We must find the way to resist. Find the way, there are always people who can understand what you are saying everywhere. One small country cannot fight alone.

Nawal El Saadawi, Egyptian writer, psychiatrist and feminist, 'Empowerment of Women, Writing and Fighting', lecture, 1981

A stone against a tank is a stone against a tank
but a bullet in a child's chest rips into the heart of
the house.

Ingrid de Kok, South African poet, 'All Wat Kind Is' (Chipasula & Chipasula, p183)

and the daughter of my father
she raised an arm to stop them ...
and all was still

Catherine Obianuju Acholonu, Nigerian poet, 'The Dissidents' (Chipasula & Chipasula, p63)

They can kill a person but not the song
When it's sung the whole world round.

Anonymous poem given to South African activist Jenny Schreiner by a fellow woman prisoner (Barbara Schreiner, p3)

... the Special Branch always came twice a month
to check on me, and they only stopped this year ...
I couldn't sleep because they were always coming
to check on me. One day I shouted at them and
started to insult them, I said, 'Hey! I'm a granny, I'm
seventy-eight years old. You fok off!' They went.

Interview with South African activist **Elizabeth Mokhele**, conducted by Barbara Schreiner on 15 May 1991, 'Where is Mandela?' *A Snake with Ice Water*, 1992, p83

How do you plead?

Guilty your Honour
Guilty
Guilty
Guilty and proud.

First verse of the poem 'For Marion Sparg', by South African
activist **Annemarie Hendrikz** (Barbara Schreiner, p45)

I have heard of a boy who said 'I'm not afraid to die
now, but when Mandela's released, *then* I'll be afraid
to die.'

Emma Mashinini, South African trade unionist, *Strikes Have
Followed Me All My Life*, 1989, p135

As I grew to love him, I understood his kind of life
– that it wasn't a normal kind of life and marrying
him was not really marrying the man ... I was
marrying the struggle.

Winnie Madikizela-Mandela, South African politician and
former wife of Nelson Mandela (*Great South Africans*, 2004,
p68)

Now you have touched the women
you have struck a rock
you have dislodged a boulder
you will be crushed.

Song of **South African women's anti-passbook campaign**,
1956 (Sharp, p115)

I have heard that you have come from over the sea,
in a ship, in order to make war on my father. Today

the victory is on your side, but luck is changeable, and if you will take my advice, you will return to your own homes; because before long, my father will come down on you like a lion, and take his revenge.

> Statement by **Margaret**, teenage daughter of Hendrik Witbooi, chief of the Kowese Hottentot people of Namibia, speaking to her German captors in April 1893, as recorded in *The Blue Book*, 1918

Responsibility

Civil society should embrace not only their rights but also their responsibilities.

> **Wangari Maathai**, Kenyan environmental and human rights activist, Nobel Lecture after receiving the Nobel Peace Prize, Oslo, Norway, 10 December 2004

The necessity of taking responsibility for one's actions represents ... a genuine power.

> **Werewere Liking**, Cameroonian playwright, interview with Michelle Mielly, Ki-Yi Village, Abidjan, Côte d'Ivoire, 2 June 2002 (African Postcolonial Literature in the Postcolonial Web)

Revenge

In giving up one's justified right to revenge, and in communicating this to the offender empathy and acceptance become evident and the offender's humanity is restored (self worth restored and guilt reduced), whether he/she responds positively or immediately or not at all. In restoring another's humanity, one's own (offended's) humanity is also restored and with it, the potential for emotional healing; restored self worth and a sense of peace.

Ginn Fourie, South African professor, whose daughter Lyndi was killed by anti-apartheid soldiers in the Heidelberg Tavern attack in Cape Town in 1993

There's nothing to be gained by any sort of personal revenge.

Shawn Slovo, South African screenwriter, 1995 interview, *Cutting Through the Mountain*, p454

Revolution

Revolution is a process. It's not done in one night. You cannot do anything in one night. And knowledge comes gradually. Like a piece of light. Because the brain sometimes is so dark. There is a thick veil on the brain. That's why we say we need to unveil the mind. So I have to understand, first, the audience to whom I am talking. And I don't believe in shock treatment ... Because when you shock people, sometimes they don't listen.

Nawal El Saadawi, Egyptian writer, psychiatrist and feminist, 'Conversation with Dr Nawal el Saadawi', interview by Stephanie McMillan, 1999

I am a useless kind of person in any liberation movement or revolution; I can't stand them or the people who organize them.

Bessie Head, South African-born Botswanan writer, *The Best of South African Short Stories*, 1991, p324

Royalty

The Malagasy had created things years and years before the colonizers came there. We had kings and queens that ruled Madagascar well before other African countries. Yet starting in the 1890s colonization buried all that. So now I ask why are we all just workers for other people? We used to do things for ourselves, and we still can. Now I'm drawing more and more to these old histories, to remind these people that we used to be strong, and we can be again. Just reading about my kings and queens gives me the energy that I need to do what I do.

Hanitra Rasoanaivo, lead singer of the Malagasy band Tarika, 'Long Way from Home', by Michal Shapiro, www.Rootsworld.com

I say that I'm a Mozambiquan not because I was Mozambiquan. I never was before the Portuguese. I was a princess of the Marraquen, where my grandfather, by my father, was the king of the state of Marraquen.

Lina Magaia, Mozambican writer, 'My Century', *BBC World Service*, 16 December 1999

Small I am like Queen Victoria; great like her I hope
to be.
   Zaudita, Empress of Ethiopia, words upon her coronation

I have restored that which had been ruined.
I have raised up that which had gone to pieces
before.
   Hatshepsut, Egyptian queen, *c.* 1540-1481 BC (Jackson, p27)

Sadness

Oh, Cape Verde, you are my sadness most sublime.
   Lyrics from a *mornas* of Cape Verdean singer **Cesaria Evora**
   ('Cesaria Evora Brings Cape Verde Music to the World', All
   Things Considered, *National Public Radio*, 12 September 1995)

... I saw her raise the corner of her apron. And I
knew that down the brown old cheeks the tears
were following each other along their accustomed
route.
   Sarah Gertrude Millin, South African writer, 'Pumpkins'
   (Dodd, p6)

'Ever seen a blind man cry, sir? It's – it's awful,
sir. Makes you feel as if something was wrong up
above.'
   Ethelreda Lewis, South African writer, 'Blind Justice', 1920s
   (Dodd, p86)

Science and Technology

The world is dominated by the few that own the money, technology and media.

Nawal El Saadawi, Egyptian novelist, psychiatrist and feminist, 'Transformation: An Informal Journal about Yari Yari Pamberi 2004', by Felicia Pride, November 2004 (www.thebacklist.net)

Technology is key to economic development ... unless Africa creates the environment for creative innovations and supports the same, she will remain technologically backward in a world where technology dominates commerce, politics and even culture.

Wangari Maathai, Kenyan environmental and human rights activist, 'Bottle-Necks of Development in Africa', paper presented at the 4th UN World Women's Conference in Beijing, China, August-September 1995

Science should integrate with philosophy; reality is not always that plain but rather complicated if not sometimes misleading and challenging.

Sameera Moussa, first Egyptian nuclear research scientist (www.iearnegypt.org)

Self-reliance

Your rescue is within you.

Lauretta Ngcobo, South African writer, quoted in the 2004 film *Belonging* (www.africaatthepictures.co.uk)

You are alone. You arrive alone and you leave alone. No one gets into the box with you when you die. Husbands come and go, children leave. Before you can depend on a man, you must be able to depend on yourself.

Rayda Jacobs, South African author, 'The Doekom', *Post-Cards from South Africa*, 2004, p37

That peace and strength come, are they not the children of the soul, and no outcome of wafer, priest, or star?

Olive Schreiner, South African writer, *Undine*, 1928 (Emslie, p177)

Sex

Sexwise, the Nigerian woman or girl child, remains a rare breed in the understanding of sexual practice … whereas it is common to find exceptions, the average Nigerian woman values sex or sexual intercourse as a tool of upward mobility, status acquisition and most importantly a ritual to appease a 'god' in the person of the opposite sex, viz, the Nigerian man. This in itself constitutes an aura of sacredness around sexual experience and that is why, in our society we still pride ourselves on values of female modesty and morality.

Remi Adedeji, Nigerian writer, 'I Love Nigeria, I No Go Lie', *The Sun News* online, 7 March 2004

I have always miscalculated the currency of sex.

Zoë Wicomb, South African writer, 'Behind the Bougainvillea', *You Can't Get Lost in Cape Town*, 1987 (Bharati Mukerjee, 'They Never Wanted to Be Themselves', *The New York Times*, 24 May 1987)

But in a society like this, which man cared to be owned and possessed when there were so many women freely available? And even all the excessive love-making was purposeless, aimless, just like tipping everything into an awful cesspit where no one really cared to take a second look.

Bessie Head, South African-born Botswanan writer, *When Rain Clouds Gather*, chapter 8, 1968 (Partnow, *The Quotable Woman*, p414)

the great sacrament of life.

South African writer **Olive Schreiner** referred to sex as such in a letter to Havelock Ellis, December 1911 (Buchanan-Gould, p200)

Sexual life forms as ever the warp on which in the loom of human life the web is woven, and runs as a thread never absent through every design and pattern of individual existence on earth.

Olive Schreiner, South African writer (Buchanan-Gould, pp227-228)

Oh, it isn't only the body of a woman that a man touches when he takes her in his hands; it's her brain, it's her intellect, it's her whole life!

Olive Schreiner, South African writer, *From Man to Man*, 1927 (Emslie, p566)

Sexism

I continue to find black men, in general, to be hostile
and non-supporting of any black woman who deems
to stand up for herself and for other women and to
be public with her politics and her life. Of course,
they support these qualities in the White man's
mother, and will stand beside and support her
in everything she does ... but not me, an African
woman.

Kola Boof, Sudanese-American writer and activist, report on
her book tour, 27 August 2004 (poetwomen.50megs.com)

The day I feel that men are getting the short end
of the stick and ... polyandry becomes the order
of the day, I'll try to start writing poems that are
sympathetic to the men folk.

Lola Shoneyin, Nigerian poet, interview with Nnorom
Azuonye, 'My E-conversation with Lola Shoneyin', *Sentinel
Poetry*, online magazine, February 2004

Women [are] melting under patriarchy. This is
because they are 'recycled' and treated in com-
mercial and sexist ways.

Sybille Ngo Nyeck, Cameroonian columnist, '(Homo)eroticism
and Calixthe Beyala', *The Witness Magazine*

I do believe that women do get the shorter end of
the deal most times and not just in Africa. I harp on
Africa because charity begins at home.

Chika Unigwe, Nigerian writer, interview with Nnorom

Azuonye, 'My E-Conversation with Chika Unigwe', *Sentinel*,
March 2003

I am angry that many societies have different rules
of conducts for women.

I am angry that Igbo proverbs that deal with
women tend to negate them (unless that woman is a
mother. What of less fecund women?)

I am angry that in Igbo societies, a male's birth
is celebrated more lavishly than a female's. That my
mother told me proudly that having given birth to
a third son in a row, an Igbo husband would have
killed a goat for me.

I am angry that someone very close to me was
sent out of her matrimonial home for having three
daughters but no son.

Chika Unigwe, Nigerian writer, interview with Nnorom
Azuonye, 'My E-Conversation with Chika Unigwe', *Sentinel*,
March 2003

Why is it they hate like this? What have I done
which makes me the sinner? Where is the man who
made my baby?

Amina Lawal, Nigerian mother who was condemned to being
stoned to death for having a child out of wedlock, article by
Anton Antonowicz, 24 August 2002, Mirror.co.uk

... the condition of women in Madagascar has
always been terrible, and I won't be silent about it!
Women are enduring a horrible plight. They have
always been considered to be lower than men, and

they have to bear 14 children, and if they don't they are considered to be worthless.

Hanitra Rasoanaivo, lead singer of the Malagasy band Tarika, 'Long Way from Home', by Michal Shapiro, www.Rootsworld. com

When I was in jail I was so convinced that when we go out, we – men and women – would build a socialist Algeria together but Algeria was built without us. We, the women, we were excluded.

Baya Hocine, Algerian journalist and independence fighter, quoted in an article in *The Middle East* magazine, Chris Kutschera, April 1996 (www.Chris-Kutschera.com)

I wonder if it will prove to have been easier to fight the oppression of apartheid than it will ever be to set women free in our societies ... Male domination does not 'burn down'.

Lauretta Ngcobo, South African writer (Bruner, *African Women's Writing*, pp94-5)

In my country, I have lowered my eyes in the presence of my father, just like my mother and my grandmother did. The men would order: take-give-do. The women would obey. That was life. In my country, the eyes of women are so sad that it seems that all the streams of Mali come to die there, bereft of hope.

Calixthe Beyala, Cameroonian novelist, *Maman a un amant*, 1993 (iupjournals.org)

The victimization, I saw, was universal. It didn't depend on poverty, on lack of education or on tradition. It didn't depend on any of the things I had thought it depended on. Men took it everywhere with them ... Femaleness as opposed and inferior to maleness.

Tsitsi Dangarembga, Zimbabwean writer, *Nervous Conditions*, 1988, pp115-16

My sister, I, who thought I'd awaken you, I'm afraid that the two of us, the three of us, all of us – except for the midwives, the mothers standing guard, the death-bearing grandmothers – will find ourselves shackled again in this 'west of the East', this corner of the earth where the dawn has risen so slowly that dusk is already settling around us on all sides.

Assia Djebar, Algerian writer and filmmaker (Colby, *World Authors 1980-1985*, p217)

The disease from which we are suffering, is the classification of the human race according to the sexual difference, which is *not* a sound basis for classification in any but purely sexual matters. We are human beings in the first place, men and women in the second.

Olive Schreiner, South African novelist, letter to Mrs Elizabeth Cobb, 1884 (Beeton, p84)

Shame

God must have had so much hope for us when he
gave us the diamonds, gold, titanium, iron, cocoa,
coffee, ginger, and palm oil ... all Sierra Leoneans,
both old and young, must feel a sense of shame for
betraying mother Sierra Leone.

> **Zainab Bangura**, head of a Sierra Leonean NGO, 'A Cry for
> Sierra Leone', *New African*, September 2001, p37

... shame kills faster than disease.

> **Buchi Emecheta**, Nigerian writer, *The Rape of Shavi*, 1985
> (Partnow, *The New Quotable Woman*, p500)

I am a woman and a woman of Africa. I am a
daughter of Nigeria and if she is in shame, I shall
stay and mourn with her in shame.

> **Buchi Emecheta**, Nigerian writer, *Destination Biafra*, 1982
> (Partnow, *The New Quotable Woman*, p500)

The heat of shame mounted through her legs and
body and sounded in her ears like the sound of sand
pouring. Pouring, pouring. She sat there, sick. A
weariness, a tastelessness, the discovery of a void
made her hands slacken their grip, atrophy emptily,
as if the hour was not worth their grasp.

> **Nadine Gordimer**, South African writer, 'The Train from
> Rhodesia', 1947 (*The Best of South African Short Stories*, 1991,
> p224)

Slavery

I assure you, the Arab man is not our brother. He is our rapist and our slave master for one thousand years in Africa. He is our devil bastard child, even worse than the white one.

Kola Boof, Sudanese-American writer and activist, 'The Africana QA: Kola Boof', interview by Jennifer Williams, 18 May 2004 (Africana website)

The Arabs and the Muslims ... are without peer the two greatest oppressors of Black African people in world history. No nation of Black men on earth have ever been more abused, more violated or more dehumanised than they have been by this thousand years of Arab Muslim racial and religious slavery, genocide and oppression. As I wrote to my beloved Amiri Baraka – If I had to choose between the Arab slavemaster and Caucasoid slavemaster – I would choose the white Caucasoid. For at least he can be impressed, seduced and mentally manipulated.

Kola Boof, Sudanese-American writer and activist, press statement, 3 January 2003 (www.kolaboof.com)

Now a woman is like a slave. She works hard. At the end of the year, the family sells one hundred bags of maize. The man gives her [about $25]. Following year the family sells three hundred bags. He still gives her [about $25.00]. What is that but slavery?

Zambian woman farmer to historian Maud Muntemba, quoted in Staudt, Kathleen, 'The Impact of Development Policies on

Women', *African Women South of the Sahara*, 1995, p229 (The African Woman Food Farmer Initiative; www.thp.org)

Grandma Mariana, my little Grandma,
smoking her gourd pipe
on the doorstep of the slave-quarters
you won't tell of your destiny ...
Alda do Espírito Santo, poet from São Tomé, 'Grandma Mariana', translated from the Portuguese by Julia Kirst (Chipasula & Chipasula, p111)

I was approximately nine years old when I, one early morning, walked around the fields, a bit far away from home, with a companion. Suddenly, we saw two strangers appear from behind a fence. One of them told my companion: 'Let the small girl go into the forest for me to pick me some fruits. Meanwhile, you continue on your walk. We'll catch up with you soon'. His objective was to fool my friend so that she wouldn't give the alarm while they were capturing me.

I, of course, did not suspect anything and hurried to obey, which my mother had accustomed me to do. Once we were in the forest, I saw two persons behind me. One of them briskly grabbed me with one hand, while the other one pulled out a knife from his belt and held it to my side. He told me 'If you cry, you'll die! Follow us!' with a lordly voice.

Josephine Bakhita, Sudanese Catholic saint (afrol News)

I, young in life, by seeming cruel fate
Was snatch'd from *Afric's* fancy'd happy seat:
What pangs excruciating must molest,
What sorrows labour in my parent's breast?
Steel'd was that soul and by no misery mov'd
That from a father seiz'd his babe belov'd.
Such, such my case. And can I then but pray
Others may never feel tyrannic sway?

Phillis Wheatley, colonial American poet brought from Africa
to America as a child-slave, 'To the Right Honourable William,
Earl of Dartmouth, His Majesty's Principal Secretary of State
for North America', 1773 (Piersen, p21)

Sleep

Open up!
Open up!
What hammered on the door of sleep?
Who's that?

Nadine Gordimer, South African writer, 'A Lion on the
Freeway', *A Soldier's Embrace*, 1975 (1983 edition, p24)

I awoke and the bridge between waking and
sleeping cracked, and there was only the aftermath
of the onslaught ...

Sheila Fugard, South African novelist and poet, *The
Castaways*, 1972 (2002 edition, p10)

Those who laugh by day sleep well.

Ethelreda Lewis, South African writer, 'Blind Justice', 1920s
(Dodd, p88)

Solitude

Yes! We think we have and know the men even as they lie beside us. But the true confidante is really the pillow. Can you imagine how many secrets we tuck in pillows … bank in pillows … impose on pillows? And I tell you, it doesn't matter whether we're male or female. It's mutual. Pillows are the real heroes …

Tess Osonye Onwueme, Nigerian playwright, 'Tell It to Women', 1997

Each man's life and struggle is a mystery, incomprehensible and forever hidden from every heart but his own.

Olive Schreiner, South African writer, *Undine*, 1928 (Emslie, p36)

What lies in a man's heart is known only to God and himself.

Pauline Smith, South African writer, 'The Schoolmaster', *The Little Karoo*, 1925 (1951 reprint, p44)

I don't think absolute solitude is good for any human creature.

Olive Schreiner, South African writer, letter from England to her husband (introduction, *The Story of an African Farm*, Penguin, 1995, p26)

Soul

I have seen some souls so compressed that they would have fitted into a small thimble, and found room to move there – wide room.

Olive Schreiner, South African writer, *The Story of an African Farm*, 1883 (Penguin, 1995, p185)

The path through life in which each soul must tread is single.

Olive Schreiner, South African writer, *Undine*, 1928 (Emslie, p36)

Oh, the things of life are very little, and the soul is great.

Olive Schreiner, South African writer, *Undine*, 1928 (Emslie, p132)

South Africa

No easy walk between perception and truth in this country.

South African poet and writer **Antjie Krog**, *A Change of Tongue*, 2003, p27

What makes this place so interesting is that it is full of paradoxes. Some people will talk about a nation of grime and crime. For others it is a rainbow nation, full of promise and reconciliation. The only thing I can tell you with certainty is this: South Africa and its people will get into your soul. You won't leave here unaffected.

Character Brenda speaking in South African **Ruth Tearle**'s organisational transformation book *Ride the Wild Tiger*, 2000, p75

Right and wrong, truth and lies are concepts that have become so confused in this country that no one will ever get them unravelled again.

Dalene Matthee, South African novelist, *The Day the Swallows Spoke*, 1992, p174

Like the inlaid, meaningless landscape photographs of the sunny South Africa which seemed to strive to create beauty in surroundings where most of the time only ugliness and cruelty prevailed.

Miriam Tlali, South African writer, 'Devil at a Dead End', 1989 (Medalie, p140)

How thankful I should be! I have had as a background for my life this wonderful South Africa, so vivid and so beautiful, though cruel at times.

Elsa Smithers, South African farmer, *March Hare*, 1935, p224

We get life here, not Hollywood.

Character speaking on South Africa in the 1920s short story 'Blind Justice', by South African writer **Ethelreda Lewis** (Dodd, p91)

… How, of our divided peoples, can a great, healthy, harmonious and desirable nation be formed? This is the final problem of South Africa. If we cannot solve it, our fate is sealed.

Olive Schreiner, South African writer, *Thoughts on South Africa*, 1923 (1992 edition, pp57-58)

South African Cities – Cape Town

Table Mountain, backdrop to the mother-city, the beautiful 'castle in rock', is a very angry mountain because he can never sleep. They shine strong lights in his eyes every night so that people can look at his beauty in the dark as well. He calls out for help, he cries out in fury, with fire after fire, but no one hears.
Dalene Matthee, South African novelist, *The Day the Swallows Spoke*, 1992, p168

Cape Town has always been a bit flaky.
Lin Sampson, South African journalist (Crwys-Williams, p320)

'You can't get lost in Cape Town. There,' and he pointed over his shoulder, 'is Table Mountain and there is Devil's Peak and there Lion's Head, so how in heaven's name could you get lost?'
Zoë Wicomb, South African writer, 'You Can't Get Lost in Cape Town', *You Can't Get Lost in Cape Town*, 1987 (Busby, p758)

… that sluggish hungry old city that is stretching out like an octopus to devour the beautiful green Peninsula.
Joy Packer, South African novelist, *Valley of the Vines*, 1955, p100

The mountain changes as often as one's moods, but whether seen in the clear radiance of a cloudless morning or through the dust and gale of a Cape south-easter, or whether only half visible in veiling mist, it is always lovely. Even at night it has its charms.

On Cape Town's Table Mountain, **Elsa Smithers**, South African farmer, *March Hare*, 1935, p149

South African Cities – Johannesburg and Soweto

The heart of the city will be reclaimed, the centre made anew, its renaissance shaped by the stubborn spirit of those who have never given up on her, never crossed her out of their lives. Cantankerous city, what will make you smile again?

Véronique Tadjo, writer from Côte d'Ivoire, 'Eyes Wide Open', *From Jo'burg to Jozi*, 2002, p233

And so, in this sprawling placeless place where glittering affluence and abject wretchedness are chained together like dead and living bodies, we are always en route, we always have places to go.

Marlene van Niekerk, South African writer, 'Take Your Body Where it has Never Been Before', *From Jo'burg to Jozi*, 2002, p243

He hated Johannesburg. He hated the constant fear that stalked him every day. He hated the daily dose of news about violence, crime, fraud and corruption. He hated the way people lived in terror behind their high walls and electrified fences. He hated the poverty, the dirt, and the litter that he saw every day on his way to work. And most of all he hated the beggars hobbling about on fake crutches at every traffic light. They were con artists – just like him.

Ruth Tearle, South African strategic planner, *Ride the Wild Tiger*, 2000, p77

In Johannesburg, what matters is what you do, how well you do it, and how much money you make.

Hilary Prendini Toffoli, South African journalist (Crwys-Williams, p323)

… the spread of shebeens and malls that splash jazz from what used to be poverty-stricken townships to the City Hall. The place we now call Soweto City. Connected by skyway and flyway, over and underground, as steady as the steel and the foreign funding on which it runs. Talk about one door closing. The Old Order was not yet cold in its grave and the place was gyrating, like a woman in love.

Maureen Isaacson, South African writer and journalist, 'Holding Back Midnight', 1992 (Medalie, p155)

… Johannesburg, rough, built on gold, as it were breathing by the power of gold, a city waxing and waning with the fortunes of gold… may be exciting, violent, vibrant, but it has no mystery, nothing for the imagination, no invisible dimensions.

Doris Lessing, English-Zimbabwean author, 'Out of the
Fountain', *The Story of a Non-Marrying Man and Other Stories*,
1972 (1990 edition, p13)

... it was an instinctive dislike of the shallow and
rather ostentatious life which I knew we should
have to lead in the Golden City ... Johannesburg has
been from the start a pleasure-loving city. Owing
to the wealth of the mines money has always been
easily earned, and the lure of gold was bound to
have an effect on the outlook of its inhabitants.
Elsa Smithers, South African farmer, *March Hare*, 1935,
pp194, 196

Johannesburg is growing more and more dreadful.
War is nothing – it's the people whom no war can
alter or change, who are so terrible.
Olive Schreiner, South African writer, around 1899
(Schoeman, p13)

South Africans

... show me a South African who hasn't suffered
some kind of identity crisis, and I'll show you
someone who's bought the plan.
Rayda Jacobs, South African author, 'For the Smell of the Sea',
Post-Cards from South Africa, 2004, p98

It ... surprises me that I could go into a riot in a
squatter camp without anybody threatening me

or being hostile toward me. I don't understand it. I think that there is something very, very special about black people in this country. People are prepared to listen to me and to judge me as a human being and not merely as someone with a white skin. It amazes me every time I experience it because I don't think that I would have that tolerance if I were in that position.

Hettie V, pseudonym for an Afrikaner journalist and activist, interview in Diana E H Russell, *Lives of Courage: Women for a New South Africa*, 1989, p295

Whenever I hear the South African accent it always sounds to me kind of practical, common-sensical and unfussy.

Janet Suzman, South African actress (Crwys-Williams, p217)

… there are things we know about each other that are never spoken, but are there to be written – and received with the amazement and consternation, on both sides, of having been found out … What's certain is that there is no representation of our social reality without that strange area of our lives in which we have knowledge of one another.

Nadine Gordimer, South African writer, 'Living in the Interregnum', *The Essential Gesture: Writing, Politics and Places*, edited by Stephen Clingman, 1988, p279 (Medalie, p xxxv)

Although Roxane nursed the image of her French mother and often tried to envisage English John Williams who had died before her birth, in spite

of her dreams of France and a somewhat fantastic
London built on 'Peter Pan in Kensington Gardens',
she regarded the Valley as her natural background
and Granny Con as the supreme authority, father
and mother rolled into one. She thought of herself as
South African and of the de Valois family as her own.
The graft had taken.

> **Joy Packer**, South African novelist, *Valley of the Vines*, 1955, p42

We are a more or less homogeneous blend of
heterogeneous social particles in different stages
of development and of cohesion with one another,
underlying and overlaying each other like the
varying strata of confused geological formations.

> **Olive Schreiner**, South African writer, *Thoughts on South
> Africa*, 1923 (1992 edition, p48)

Success and Failure

You may not succeed, and it may fail. You need to
look at it and say, were you being true to yourself in
doing it? And even though you knew it would fail,
would you do it again?

> **Gill Marcus**, South African politician, 1995 interview, *Cutting
> Through the Mountain*, p264

Just keep trying and trying. If you have the determi-
nation and commitment you will succeed.

> **Buchi Emecheta**, Nigerian writer, interview with Julie
> Holmes, *The Voice*, 9 July 1996

Has not the victor's fate been, from the beginning,
to lie down and weep?

Olive Schreiner, South African writer, *Undine*, 1928 (Emslie, p35)

The surest sign of fitness is success.

Olive Schreiner, South African writer, *The Story of an African Farm*, 1883 (Penguin, 1995, p193)

Suffering

Her mother said nothing. She never said anything. She washed and cooked and cleaned and took on all the insults like the layers and layers of fat creeping slowly up on her hips and thighs.

Rayda Jacobs, South African author, 'The Pantie', *Post-Cards from South Africa*, 2004, p27

If life is a series of joys and pains, the joys are fleeting, but the pains, even if forgotten, sometimes leave marks, even scars.

Orlanda Amarílis, Cape Verdean writer, 'Maira da Luz *Literary Review*, Summer 1995, translated by Gerald M Moser (internet: looksmart/find articles)

I met a woman the other day whom I'd not seen for a long time and the first thing she said to me was, 'Aren't you glad to hear that the Kaiser's got cancer?' Now what could I say? I've had much too much physical suffering to rejoice in the suffering of any sentient creature: if a lion had torn my arm off I wouldn't want it to have cancer. There would be its physical suffering added to my physical suffering, to make the terrible sum total of suffering bigger! I think I can understand most things in human nature, but delight in human suffering (or animal) I cannot understand.

Olive Schreiner, South African writer, letter to Adela Smith, December 1916 (www.spartacus.schoolnet.co.uk)

Once God Almighty said: 'I will produce a self-working automatic machine for enduring suffering, which shall be capable of the largest amount of suffering in a given space;' and he made woman.

Olive Schreiner, South African writer, letter to Havelock Ellis, 9 November 1888 (Buchanan-Gould, p95)

Teaching

I love teaching. I love the cool things that come out of literature and film study, the bizarre historical facts that make you go, 'Goddamn! I didn't know that!' That makes all the difference.

Diane Awerbuck, South African writer, 'It's Not About the Therapy', by Nils van der Linden, 27 January 2005 (iafrica.com)

My feeling of exile, of being an 'alien' disappeared every time I entered my class and looked in the eyes of my students. They reminded me of the eyes of young women and men at home, of the eyes of my daughter and son. They reminded me of the eyes I saw in the mirror when I was a medical student in Cairo university during the fifties, and when I was a post-graduate student in Columbia university in New York during the sixties.

Nawal El Saadawi, Egyptian writer, psychiatrist and feminist, 'Exile and Resistance', Cairo, November 2002

When we stood in front of our over-crowded class-rooms, we represented a force in the enormous effort to be accomplished in order to overcome ignorance.

Mariama Bâ, Senegalese writer, *So Long a Letter*, 1979 (1981 edition, p23)

An army without drums, without gleaming uniforms. This army, thwarting traps and snares, everywhere plants the flag of knowledge and morality.

Mariama Bâ, Senegalese writer, *So Long a Letter*, 1979 (1981 edition, p23)

Time

'Just now' and 'now now' can mean anything from two hours to two weeks into the future. 'In a minute' can mean in a day – as in 'he's just gone out for a minute'. This means he might not be back until the following day.

Description of South African time in *The How-to-Be a South African Handbook*, by South African writers **Marianne Thamm** and Toby Newsome, 2002, p82

Another week gone, another day gone. What have you done? We never come back, we moments; we fly, but we never return, never, never, tick, tick. What have you done with us? If you do the best you can with all the rest of us, you can never bring one of us back, never, never, tick, tick.

Olive Schreiner, South African writer, *Undine*, 1928 (Emslie, p6)

Travel

The title 'United Kingdom' when pronounced by Adah's father sounded so heavy, like the type of noise one associated with bombs. It was so deep, so mysterious, that Adah's father always voiced it in hushed tones, wearing such a respectful expression as if he were speaking of God's Holiest of Holies. Going to the United Kingdom must surely be like paying God a visit. The United Kingdom, then, must be like heaven.

Buchi Emecheta, Nigerian writer, *The Second-Class Citizen*, 1975 (Colby, *World Authors 1975-1980*, p212)

I ... have learnt to peruse maps, and they tell so little.

Sheila Fugard, South African novelist and poet, *The Castaways*, 1972 (2002 edition, p17)

It is customary to ridicule the traveller who passes rapidly through a country, and then writes his impression of it. The truth is he sees much that is hidden for ever from the eyes of the inhabitants. Habit and custom have blinded them.

Olive Schreiner, South African writer, *Thoughts on South Africa*, 1923 (1976 Africana Book Society reprint, p28)

Tribalism

I have never seen a light blinking on a child's forehead saying 'I'm Hutu', or 'I'm Tutsi'. When I see a child, I see a child. If he's Tutsi, he's Tutsi. If he's Hutu, he's Hutu. He's a child and, above all, a Burundian.

Esther Kamatari, Burundian princess and former fashion model, interview with Associated Press Television News regarding her presidential candidacy ('Burundian Princess for President', www.news.24.com, edited by Tori Foxcroft, 24 December 2004)

The threat of a more open political system and a strong civil society has disquieted enough African leaders and has forced them to encourage the brewing of tribal tensions the worst of which was the recent violence which ravaged Rwanda and Somalia. It is important to emphasize that it is not the tribes who want to fight, rather, it is the threatened elitist leaders who are using tribes to arouse ethnic nationalism as the only way they can continue to cling to political and economic power and the privileges which that power comes with. Such leaders speak peace while they are planning civil wars.

Wangari Maathai, Kenyan environmental and human rights activist, 'Bottle-Necks of Development in Africa', paper presented at the 4th UN World Women's Conference in Beijing, China, August-September 1995

Where one was born is
most important. Especially when
we
tell
you
so.

Ama Ata Aidoo, Ghanaian writer, 'From the Only Speech That Was Not Delivered At the Rally' (Reed and Wake, p1)

Truth

perched on your cousin's roof
truth falls as fast as stars

Toyin Adewale-Gabriel, Nigerian writer, 'A Tale of Two Vultures (as told after the Owerri riots),' *Sentinel Poetry*, online magazine, November 2003

The truth is reached through dispute, robust debate and the occasional clip around the ear.

South African writer and journalist **Marianne Thamm**, 'Dead or living in Canada', 9 May 2001 (*Mental Floss*, 2002, p17)

The truth, like a good burp after a succulent steak, will out.

South African writer and journalist **Marianne Thamm**, 'Life's a bitch (and then they eat you)', 7 April 2001 (*Mental Floss*, 2002, p8)

Talk with a free heart and your message will be true.
Words of a female sangoma, speaking in South African **Ruth Tearle**'s organisational transformation book *Ride the Wild Tiger*, 2000, p227

Right and wrong, truth and untruth are streams that have run together, forming one roaring, swelling river. No matter where you put your bucket in, the water you draw up is never pure.
Dalene Matthee, South African novelist, *The Day the Swallows Spoke*, 1992, p9

Truth is a deception that changes to falsehood while you finger it.
Olive Schreiner, South African writer, *Undine*, 1928 (Emslie, p154)

There is no small truth – all truth is great! ... Whether the truth concerns the feathers on a pigeon's wing or the constitution of a lump of earth or a psychological fact, we know that it is vital.
Olive Schreiner, South African writer, *From Man to Man*, 1927 (Emslie, p506)

It never pays the Man who speaks the truth, but it pays Humanity that it should be spoken.
Olive Schreiner, South African writer, *Letters*, 1924 (Buchanan-Gould, p153)

All things on earth have their price; and for truth we pay the dearest ... on the path to truth, at every step you set your foot down on your heart.

Olive Schreiner, South African writer, *The Story of an African Farm*, 1883 (Penguin, 1995, p148)

United States-Africa relations

That's how it was in apartheid South Africa.

I recognize that bullying when Cheney, Ashcroft, Bush and others say that anyone who votes for Kerry is inviting another attack from al-Qaida. How do they know? Are they talking to Osama? Is this what the intelligence agencies report to the White House?

Bush supporters accuse Kerry, and any one else with a question or dissent, of giving comfort to the enemy, in other words, of being a traitor ...

Perhaps I fear too much, but I am a grandmother. I want my grandchildren to grow up in a decent America. I left a state where every prison groaned with torture. Now I fear that the America I love is falling to hooligans like those I left.

Rose Rappoport Moss, South African writer, 'A New Set of Hooligans to Fear', *The Anniston Star*, 30 September 2004

Black America hates the black woman in her authentic form. They want a woman who can reflect the whiteness they covet. They fear anyone who highlights or questions their self-hatred. They've always dreamt of some glorious Egyptian or Ethiopian queen ... but I am a disappointment, you see, I am not at all what they imagined their Nile River goddess would be like. One journalist said that I'm a cross between Alice Walker, Madonna and Grace Jones. Just horrifying!

> **Kola Boof**, Sudanese-American writer and activist, on why she has not been embraced by the black American press, 'The Africana QA: Kola Boof', interview by Jennifer Williams, 18 May 2004 (Africana website)

As unfashionable as it may be, let me say God Bless America. Because if it weren't for freedom of speech and freedom of self-determination for women and freedom to vote and create my life's ART ... then I would surely go mad.

> **Kola Boof**, Sudanese-American writer and activist, press statement, 3 January 2003 (www.kolaboof.com)

There is a new phrase in the air, and it hurts my ear like a sour note: 'constructive engagement'. This is Washington's way of saying, 'Speak softly and do not even carry a stick, and maybe everything will get better.'

> **Miriam Makeba**, South African singer and civil rights activist, *Makeba, My Story*, 1988, p233

Violence

In Liberia, our security do not shoot you ... They pluck (out) your eyes, they cut off your ears, and they cut out your tongue.

> **Suzana Vaye**, widow of murdered Liberian deputy minister of public works, Issac Nuhan Vaye ('Alleged Liberian Coup Leaders Killed', 16 July 2003, UN Wire)

Violence is always the consequence of hurt and shame.

> **Ginn Fourie**, South African professor, whose daughter Lyndi was killed by anti-apartheid soldiers in the Heidelberg Tavern attack in Cape Town in 1993, article in *Huisgenoot* & *You* magazines, 2003

Once grouped around an act of violence, anything and everything becomes suspicious.

> **Nadine Gordimer**, South African writer, *The House Gun*, 1998 (1999 paperback, p31)

Violence against women and children

'28 stupid men'

> How South African actress **Charlize Theron** characterised those who criticised a controversial anti-rape TV campaign in South Africa ('Out of Africa', Emma Brockes, *The Guardian*, 2 April 2004, http://film.guardian.co.uk)

When he first beat me up (with a snake stick), the police only arrived to ask him to 'do it more quietly'.

> **Kola Boof**, Sudanese-American writer and activist, press statement, 3 January 2003 (www.kolaboof.com)

Africa has a repressed memory. Why is there so much silence in Africa? If African women started remembering all of the violence that they experienced, well, it would be an explosion. Is this really a good thing? I'm not so sure. I believe that they succeed in killing the event by silence, and perhaps in our case it's for the better.

Werewere Liking, Cameroonian playwright, interview with Michelle Mielly, Ki-Yi Village, Abidjan, Côte d'Ivoire, 2 June 2002 (African Postcolonial Literature in the Postcolonial Web)

In South Africa, the sad thing is that the vagina is the scene of the crime.

South African writer and journalist **Marianne Thamm**, 'Read our lips', 8 May 2002 (*Mental Floss*, 2002, p88)

Every 26 seconds in South Africa, a woman gets raped. It was my turn last Thursday night.

Charlene Smith, South African journalist and anti-rape activist, 'One Woman's Crusade Against Rape in S. Africa', *The Christian Science Monitor*, by Corinna Schuler, 4 December 2000

In the early 1980s, MPs were discussing the length of the stick that men should be allowed to use in order to beat their wives.

Louisa Ait-Hamou, Algerian activist, 'Women's Struggle Against Muslim Fundamentalism in Algeria: Strategies or a Lesson For Survival?' (www.whrnet.org)

Wife battering and circumcision are violations of human rights but very few people want to declare them violations of human rights; if you are beaten you are both physically and psychologically abused yet it is not considered an abuse of human rights! These issues should be looked at as political issues not cultural issues. If we continue viewing them as cultural issues people will say they cannot intervene in our culture and we will continue being oppressed.

Hope Chigudu, Vice-Chairperson, Zimbabwe Women's

Resource Centre and Network, quoted in Getecha, Ciru and Chipika, Jesimen, *Zimbabwe Women's Voices*, 1995, p77 (The African Woman Food Farmer Initiative; www.thp.org)

The bandit chief of the group picked out one, the small girl who was less than eight. In front of everyone, he tried to rape her. The child's vagina was small and he could not penetrate. On a whim, he took a whetted pocketknife and opened her with a violent stroke. He took her in blood. The child died.

Lina Magaia, Mozambican writer, *Dumba Nengue: Run for Your Life*, 1987, p20 ('Frelimo: thirty years of fighting for a free Mozambique – Mozambique Liberation Front', by Joseph Reilly, *Monthly Review*, October 1992)

We shouldn't speak about violence against women separate from politics, nationally, internationally. The family is the unit of the society. When there is violence inside the family; it is a reflection of violence in the state, when there is violence in the state; it is a reflection of violence in the whole world.

Nawal El Saadawi, Egyptian writer, psychiatrist and feminist, 'Empowerment of Women, Writing and Fighting', lecture, 1981

Our land has become a land in which we must guard our thighs
Like a man guarding crops from birds.

Dinka girl sings of a man who forced unwanted sex upon her (Deng, p92)

War

Women talk about their losses and how to rebuild.
Men talk about their guns and how to keep their
machinery intact.

> **Zainab Hawa Bangura**, Sierra Leonean politician, 'Women are
> Critical for Building the Peace, Says Kennedy School Panel', by
> Miranda Daniloff Mancusi, Harvard News, 5 November 2003
> (www.ksg.harvard.edu)

What do we want? What is it that is so important
that we are fighting for? If it is in the interest of the
people then there should be no fighting.

> **Ruth Perry**, Former Interim Head of State of Liberia, speaking
> at ECOWAS-led peace talks in August 2003 in Ghana ('We
> Wonna Go Home! – The Liberian Story', by Nana Kodjo Jehu-
> Appiah, 29 August 2003, GNA)

If you can mobilize resources for war, why can't you
mobilize resources for life?

> **Graça Machel**, Mozambican educator and politician (as
> quoted by Kofi Annan on 9 December 2002 during an address
> upon receipt of an honorary doctorate from the University of
> Cape Town)

This is the map of a war: territories, frontiers and
sprawling craters are inscribed in black and white
– it is the map of a new world. Children slide along
this map with little speed cars made of tin cans,
their bodies puffed by the wind, navigating the
world to its farthest limits.

Ana Paula Taveres, Angolan poet, 'Kuito, A Child's Map
of War and Infinity – Photographs and Poetry Regarding
Angolan Conflict', *UNESCO Courier*, July 2001

When I got home
from the war
I realised
our tradition had not changed
We were still second to men
being told
what to do

Excerpt from the poem 'Independence', credited to the
Danhiko Women's Group, Zimbabwe (*WorldViews*, 1997)

When she had looked into the well she had seen the
heads of dead people staring at her as if pleading for
help ... And the well had seemed pregnant to her.

Lina Magaia, Mozambican writer, 'The Pregnant Well',
Dumba nengue: histórias trágicas do banditismo, 1987 [Dumba
Nengue, Run For Your Life: Peasant Tales of Tragedy in
Mozambique, 1988]

You've seen our country. Now you know why we
want to be free. The Ethiopians came, they bombed
our villages, they slaughtered our cattle and burned
our children. Everything is burning now. Even the
stones are burning.

Mama Zeinab, Eritrean woman quoted in the film 'Even
the Stones are Burning', Freedom from Hunger Campaign,
Sydney, 1985

there are no more coffins
wrap it up wrap it up in a mat
> **Catherine Obianuju Acholonu**, Nigerian writer and poet, 'Harvest of War' (Chipasula & Chipasula, p65)

Sons walked out of the clearing of mud huts; past the chief's house; past the children playing ... The children called out, Where are you going? The young men didn't answer and they hadn't come back.
> **Nadine Gordimer**, South African writer, 'Oral History', *A Soldier's Embrace*, 1975 (1983 edition, p135)

Anyone who has been in, or near, war ... knows that time – a week, days, sometimes hours – when everything falls apart, when all forms of order dissolve, including those which mark the difference between enemy and enemy.
> **Doris Lessing**, English-Zimbabwean author, 'Out of the Fountain', *The Story of a Non-Marrying Man and Other Stories*, 1972 (1990 edition, p19)

It's when war comes to your own land that its full horror bursts on you.
> **Olive Schreiner**, South African writer, letter to Havelock Ellis (Buchanan-Gould, p231)

The worst of war is not the death on the battle fields; it's the meanness, the cowardice, the hatred, it awakens ... War draws out all that is basest in the human heart.
> **Olive Schreiner**, South African writer, in a letter to Emily Hobhouse (Buchanan-Gould, p232)

Hell is *Martial Law*.
> **Olive Schreiner**, South African writer, to Alf Mattison, 1901
> (Barash, p1)

WHO GAINS BY WAR? There are some who think they gain. In the background we catch sight of misty figures; we know the old tread; we hear the rustle of paper, passing from hand to hand, and we hear the clink of gold – it is an old, familiar sound in Africa. There are some who think they will gain. WHAT will they gain?
> **Olive Schreiner**, South African writer, *An English South African's View of the Situation*, 1899 (Buchanan-Gould, p173)

Wealth

This notion that everyone somehow deserves to be a millionaire, nay, is entitled to fabulous wealth and luxury, is dangerously delusional ... Whatever happened to the notion of just earning an ordinary income and living within one's means?
> South African writer and journalist **Marianne Thamm**, 'Wonderland', 10 October 2001 (*Mental Floss*, 2002, p47)

The vast majority of women (and men) do not have the luxury of any sort of choice when it comes to 'having it all'. We're damn lucky if we 'just get some'.
> South African writer and journalist **Marianne Thamm**, 'Let's hear it for superwoman', 24 July 2002 (*Mental Floss*, 2002, p104)

It often seems to me that on one side in life stands
all heroism, beauty, truth ... and on the other side,
wealth.

> **Olive Schreiner**, South African writer, letter to Mrs Brown
> written from St Dominic's Convent, 10 April 1886 (Buchanan-
> Gould, p93)

Weariness

Tru's god Lizi
I'm tired
Washing clothes for
Forty years!

> **Lindiwe Mabuza**, South African poet, 'Tired Lizi Tired'
> (Chipasula & Chipasula, p200)

I only rest
When everyone has retired.

> **M Sandasi**, Zimbabwean poet, from her poem 'My Day',
> in Getecha, Ciru and Chipika, Jesimen, *Zimbabwe Women's
> Voices*, 1995, p57 (The African Woman Food Farmer Initiative;
> www.thp.org)

At night I feel completely exhausted, as if someone
had been beating me.

> **Mariama Boubacar**, farmer from Niger, 'Women's Work:
> Africa's Precious Resource', The Hunger Project, September
> 1992, pp17, 21 (The African Woman Food Farmer Initiative;
> www.thp.org)

Our life is so hard that some days we just want to scream, to tell the world our troubles, to weep.

Mahabara Siré, farmer from Burkina Faso, 'Women's Work: Africa's Precious Resource', The Hunger Project, September 1992, pp17, 21 (The African Woman Food Farmer Initiative; www.thp.org)

I was tired, very tired; tired with a tiredness that seemed older than the heat of the day and the shining of the sun on the bricks of the Roman road ...

Olive Schreiner, South African writer, 'In a Ruined Chapel', Alassio, Italy, 1887 (Clayton, p72)

Wisdom

Wisdom never kicks at the iron walls it can't bring down.

Olive Schreiner, South African writer, *The Story of an African Farm*, 1883 (Penguin, 1995, p188)

Through wisdom I have dived down into the great sea, and have seized in the place of her depths a pearl whereby I am rich. I went down like the great iron anchor whereby men anchor ships for the night on the high seas, and I received a lamp which lighteth me, and I came up by the ropes of the boat of understanding.

Makeda, Queen of Sheba, 10th-century BC Ethiopian queen, *Kebra Negast (The Glory of the Kings)*, a 14th-century chronicle of Ethiopia's Solomonic dynasty (Busby, p16)

Women

It hasn't been de-habilitating being a woman, but it's certainly been a challenge. It is true that men don't always hear women, so you have to say things several times.

Maganthrie Pillay, South African filmmaker, 'Creating, Above All Else', by Nils van der Linden, 13 January 2005 (iafrica.com)

Women are the rock bottom of society, of the family unit, of the home, the connective tissue of society, the mainstay of economic life, the producers and reproducers. They shoulder 90% of all the work but own only 10% of what is owned. Women on the move will change the world, will give birth to another world.

Nawal El Saadawi, Egyptian writer, psychiatrist and feminist, 'Waging War on the Mind', Cairo, 11 January 2004, paper written for the World Social Forum, 2004

I got to internalize that 'nwanyi' (being a woman) didn't mean there were things you could not do.

Chimamanda Ngozi Adichie, Nigerian novelist, quoted in 'In the Footsteps of Chinua Achebe: Enter Chimamanda Ngozi Adichie, Nigeria's Newest Literary Voice', by Ike Anya, *Sentinel Poetry*, online magazine, November 2003

The average woman takes care of everyone else but herself.

Inonge Mbikusita-Lewanika, Zambian diplomat, quoted in 'Aid for Girls Going Beyond Schoolhouse', by Lori Nitschke, WOMENSENEWS, 19 October 2003

Women are responsible for their children, they cannot sit back, waste time and see them starve.

Wangari Maathai, Kenyan environmental and human rights activist (www.brainyquote.com)

Women, only women, have this sort of resource. They think of how to ameliorate.

Nadine Gordimer, South African writer, *The House Gun*, 1998 (1999 paperback, p29)

bottom power

Nigerian term for women's ability to use their sexuality – in this case a big buttocks – to get their own way (Mazrui, p128)

I feel the revolutionizing of our continent hinges on the woman question.

Ama Ata Aidoo, Ghanaian writer, 1986 interview with Adeola James (ed.), *In Their Own Voices: African Women Writers Talk*, 1990, p26

It is delightful to be a woman; but every man thanks the Lord devoutly that he isn't one.

Olive Schreiner, South African writer, *The Story of an African Farm*, 1883 (Penguin, 1995, p187)

Men are like the earth and we are the moon; we turn always one side to them, and they think there is no other, because they don't see it – but there is.

Olive Schreiner, South African writer, *The Story of an African Farm*, 1883 (Penguin, 1995, p199)

The man is the peak of the house;
That is what we have understood.

It is the women who make the pinnacle
On top of the roof.

Bemba of Zambia girls initiation song (Doob, p26)

Work

Everybody needs to get up and work!

Nahawa Doumbia, Malian singer, interview with Kristell
Diallo, March 2001, New York (Afropop Worldwide)

The difference between a person who is self-
employed and employed is that a self-employed
person works 20 hours a day in order to make the
same money as another person but in order to have
their own freedoms.

Nina Romm, South African artist (Crwys-Williams, p212)

A life's spent guarding. What there is to guard
is not the question …

Marjorie Oludhe Macgoye, Kenyan poet, 'August the First:
The Watchman Speaks' (Maja-Pearce, p10)

Kanyariri, Village of Toil,
Village of unending work.

Opening lines of 'The Village' by Kenyan playwright **Marina
Gashe** (The African Woman Food Farmer Initiative; www.thp.
org)

'Kaffir work! What's kaffir work? That's why you've
never built up a strong white proletariat, that's why

you've got a class of poor unemployable whites.
Have you never heard of the dignity of labour? Look
at these hands! I've never been ashamed of what
you call kaffir work ...'

Rose Zwi, South African novelist, *Another Year in Africa*, 1980,
p136

One would say: 'I am a clerk in the white man's
office.' Another one said: 'I am a petrol attendant.'
While a third laughed: 'I am a bread boy. I deliver to
white homes.' Always the story; their jobs were like
nooses about their necks.

Sheila Fugard, South African novelist and poet, *The
Castaways*, 1972 (2002 edition, p48)

My brother, cut me another drink. Any form of work
is work ... is work ... is work.

Character named Mansa speaking about prostitution, **Ama
Ata Aidoo**, Ghanaian writer, 'In the Cutting of a Drink', *No
Sweetness Here*, 1970 (1995 edition, p37)

Is not all work, if it be earnestly done, noble and
ennobling? Is not all labour worship, be it only
scraping a carrot or ironing a shirt?

Olive Schreiner, South African writer, *Undine*, 1928 (Emslie,
p138)

Writers

It's like being an athlete. Some of it is talent: most of
it is training.

Diane Awerbuck, South African writer, 'It's Not About the Therapy', by Nils van der Linden, 27 January 2005 (iafrica. com)

Writing is something you do, not something you are. And anyway, why are we obsessed with 'knowing' someone? It's a crock. You can trust someone's opinions without stalking them or cataloguing their every detail.

Diane Awerbuck, South African writer, 'It's Not About the Therapy', by Nils van der Linden, 27 January 2005 (iafrica. com)

I always wanted to be a writer, but once Osama bin Laden slapped me across the mouth for saying that women could write books just as well as men. He wanted me to be Nefertiti and I wanted to be Alice Walker.

Kola Boof, Sudanese-American writer and activist, 'The Africana QA: Kola Boof', interview by Jennifer Williams, 18 May 2004 (Africana website)

I think that is something about writers. They have a shaky identity. A lot of the writers I've met are in some sense outsiders. They come from another place.

Barbara Trapido, South African-born British novelist, 'Voices in Her Head', by Lin Sampson, *Sunday Times*, 9 March 2003

Writing, like music, runs in families. It is nothing special, it is genetic. Some families can cook, others can write.

Antjie Krog, South African poet and writer, *A Change of Tongue*, 2003, p112

I started writing because I realized that I had not seen myself in literature, and I wanted to see myself.
Tsitsi Dangarembga, Zimbabwean writer, introduction to *Nervous Conditions*, 1988 (2001 edition, p x)

The first book I wrote was *The Bride Price* which was a romantic book, but my husband burnt the book when he saw it. I was the typical African woman, I'd done this privately, I wanted him to look at it, approve it and he said he wouldn't read it. And later he burnt the book and I think by that time this urge to write had become more important to me than he realised, and that was the day I said I'm going to leave this marriage and he said, 'What for, that stupid book?' and I said, 'I just feel you just burn my child.'
Buchi Emecheta, Nigerian writer (BBC World Service website)

A stressed and difficult childhood often produces writers because what such a childhood does is to teach children to be very aware and to observe everything and this is of course what you need to be a writer.
Doris Lessing, English-Zimbabwean author (BBC World Service website)

... preserve the writing while their men wage war in the sun or dance before the fires at night ...

On women's role as caretakers of words, **Assia Djebar**,
Algerian novelist, *So Vast the Prison*, 1995

I suppose the truth is that really exceptional writers
have an almost morbid modesty, preserving a strict
silence about themselves and their work which
means everything to them.
  Lyndall Gregg, niece of South African writer Olive Schreiner,
  Memories of Olive Schreiner, 1957, p42

And the author says, 'Damn you, take it or leave it,
as you like!'
  Olive Schreiner, South African writer, *From Man to Man*, 1927
  (Emslie, p700)

Writing

Good reading is good writing's teacher.
  Charlotte Bauer, South African journalist, 'Opinion:
  Plagiarism Isn't Ambiguous; It's Just Theft, Plain And Simple',
  Sunday Times (Johannesburg), 7 February 2005

Never believe anything you read in a book, even if
it actually happened. It's impossible ever to retell
things accurately. Most of us piece together our
pasts in a way that will not make us insane with
guilt and regret. We have to live with ourselves.
  Diane Awerbuck, South African writer, 'It's Not About the
  Therapy', by Nils van der Linden, 27 January 2005 (iafrica.
  com)

Writing can be an abusive husband

Diane Awerbuck, South African writer, 'It's Not About the Therapy', by Nils van der Linden, 27 January 2005 (iafrica. com)

I believe everyone should operate with a sense of social responsibility. So much so that people who don't have anything positive to contribute to their environments annoy me. Everyone has something to give. I feel that writers especially owe it to their 'people' to sensitise, educate and enlighten them. Most importantly, where they can, they should speak for those who have no voice or who are hoarse and need someone to take over from them.

Lola Shoneyin, Nigerian poet, interview with Nnorom Azuonye, 'My E-conversation with Lola Shoneyin', *Sentinel Poetry*, online magazine, February 2004

I do not believe in being prescriptive about literature. I don't think writers SHOULD write this or write that. They should just write.

Chimamanda Ngozi Adichie, Nigerian novelist, quoted in 'In the Footsteps of Chinua Achebe: Enter Chimamanda Ngozi Adichie, Nigeria's Newest Literary Voice', by Ike Anya, *Sentinel Poetry*, online magazine, November 2003

No writer writes solely from personal experience. The quality of your research and the literary powers of evocation ensures credibility.

Toyin Adewale-Gabriel, Nigerian writer, from 'My E-Conversation with Toyin Adewale-Gabriel', by Nnorom Azuonye, *Sentinel Poetry*, online magazine, November 2003

It's a bit like dancing. It's about balance and stylising.

Barbara Trapido, South African-born British novelist, 'Voices in Her Head', by Lin Sampson, *Sunday Times*, 9 March 2003

I do not separate between writing and fighting.

Nawal El Saadawi, Egyptian writer, psychiatrist and feminist, 'Conversation with Dr Nawal el Saadawi', interview by Stephanie McMillan, 1999

In so many great literatures of the world, women are nearly always around to service the great male heroes. Since I am a woman it is natural that I not only write about women but with women in more central roles.

Ama Ata Aidoo, Ghanaian writer (BBC World Service website)

Fiction has a vital social responsibility.

Buchi Emecheta, Nigerian writer, interview with Julie Holmes, *The Voice*, 9 July 1996

[a] release for all my anger, all my bitterness, my disappointments, my questions and my joy

On writing, **Buchi Emecheta**, Nigerian writer, interview with Julie Holmes, *The Voice*, 9 July 1996

It is as thrilling as a lover's hot kiss to have fixed on paper something that has looked beautiful to us.

Olive Schreiner, South African writer, *Undine*, 1928 (Emslie, p107)

Zimbabwe

Bread queues, forex blues, and bloodsucking
moneylenders – that's the tale of Harare.

> **Helen Muchimba**, Zambian-based journalist, 'Going
> Downhill', *BBC Focus on Africa* magazine, April-June 2003, p31

Old Bob from up north said Ho, hum,
About England I care not a crumb.
For I hate Tony Blair
And need never go there
As long as my groceries still come.

> **Yvonne Redfern-Duff**, winner of the Hogarth Inaugural
> Robert Mugabe Zimerick Competition, 16 February 2003,
> *Sunday Times* (Johannesburg)

Rhodesia has more history stuffed into its make-
believe, colonial-dream borders than one country the
size of a very large teapot should be able to amass in
less than a hundred years. Without cracking.

> **Alexandra Fuller**, British journalist and writer who grew up
> in Zimbabwe, *Don't Let's Go to the Dogs Tonight*, 2003, p153

Yet still it would be
The same familiar beautiful Zimbabwe.

> Last lines of the poem 'After the Rain', **Kristina Rungano**,
> Zimbabwean poet (Chipasula & Chipasula, p214)

A landscape with very few human things to dot it.

> Description of where she grew up in Zimbabwe (then
> Southern Rhodesia), **Doris Lessing**, English-Zimbabwean
> author (*The Best of South African Short Stories*, 1991, p234)

Sources

Aidoo, Ama Ata. *Changes: A Love Story*. New York: The Feminist Press, 1993.

Aidoo, Ama Ata. *No Sweetness Here*. New York: The Feminist Press, 1995. [original copyright 1970]

Aidoo, Ama Ata. *Our Sister Killjoy Or, Reflections from a Black-Eyed Squint*. UK: Longman, 1977.

Awerbuck, Diane. *Gardening at Night*. London: Secker & Warburg, 2003.

Ayittey, George B N. *Africa Betrayed*. New York: St. Martin's Press, 1992.

Bâ, Mariama. *So Long A Letter*. Heinemann: 1981.

The Best of South African Short Stories. Cape Town: The Reader's Digest Association South Africa, 1991.

Beeton, Ridley. *Facets of Olive Schreiner*. Craighall, South Africa: AD Donker, 1987.

Bloom, Harold (ed.). *Doris Lessing*. New York: Chelsea House Publishers, 1986.

Bruner, Charlotte H. *African Women's Writing*. Oxford: Heinemann, 1993.

Bruner, Charlotte H. *Unwinding Threads, Writing by Women in Africa*. London: Heinemann, 1983.

Bryan, G McLeod. *Whither Africa?* Richmond, Virginia: John Knox Press, 1961.

Buchanan-Gould, Vera. *Not Without Honour, The Life and Writings of Olive Schreiner*. Cape Town: Hutchinson & Co. Ltd., 1949.

Bugul, Ken. *The Abandoned Baobab*. New York: Lawrence Hill Books, 1991. [first published 1984, Dakar, Senegal]

Busby, Margaret. *Daughters of Africa*. New York: Pantheon Books, 1992.

Calder, Argus, et al (eds). *Summer Fires: New Poetry of Africa*. Oxford: Heinemann, 1983.

Chapman, F Spencer. *Lightest Africa*. London: Chatto & Windus, 1955.

Chipasula, Stella and Frank. *The Heinemann Book of African Women's Poetry*. Oxford: Heinemann, 1995.

Christie, Iain. *Samora Machel*. London: Panaf, Zed Press Ltd., 1989.

Clayton, Cherry (ed.). *Olive Schreiner - The Woman's Rose, Stories and Allegories*. Craighall: AD Donker Publisher, 1986.

Colby, Vineta (ed.). *World Authors 1975-1980*. New York: The H.W. Wilson Co., 1985.

Colby, Vineta (ed.). *World Authors 1980-1985*. New York: The H.W. Wilson Co., 1991.

Copage, Eric V. *Black Pearls, Daily Meditations, Affirmations, and Inspirations for African-Americans*. New York: William Morrow, 1993.

Courtemanche, Gil. *A Sunday at the Pool in Kigali*. (Translated by Patricia Claxton.) Edinburgh, Scotland: Canongate, 2004.

Crwys-Williams, Jennifer. *The Penguin Dictionary of South African Quotations*. London: Penguin Books, 1994.

Dangarembga, Tsitsi. *Nervous Conditions*. London: The Women's Press Classic edition, 2001. [first published 1988]

De Villiers, Les, with Gary Player and Chris Barnard. *The Travel Guide to South Africa*. Connecticut: Business Books International, 1992.

Deng, Francis Mading. *The Dinka of the Sudan*. Illinois: Waveland Press, 1972.

Dodd, A D (ed.). *Short Stories by South African Writers*. Cape Town: Juta and Company Limited, Third Impression.

Doob, Leonard (ed.). *Ants Will Not Eat Your Fingers*. New York: Walker, 1966.

Emecheta, Buchi. *The Joys of Motherhood*. London: Heinemann, 1979.

Emslie, T S (ed.). *Olive Schreiner – Karoo Moon: Undine, The Story of An African Farm, From Man to Man*. Cape Town: Stonewall Books, 2004.

Fogg, Jeremy. *The Schreiner House Cradock*. Grahamstown: National English Literary Museum, 1993.

Fugard, Sheila. *The Castaways*. Jeppestown, South Africa: AD Donker Publishers, 2002. [first published 1972]

Fuller, Alexandra. *Don't Let's Go to the Dogs Tonight: An African Childhood*. London: Picador, 2003. [first published 2002, Random House, New York]

Gardner, John M. *Between the Thunder and the Sun, An Anthology of Short Stories*. Cape Town: Oxford University Press, 1983.

Gordimer, Nadine. *A Soldier's Embrace*. Harmondsworth: Penguin Books, 1983.

Gordimer, Nadine. *Jump and Other Stories*. Cape Town; London: D. Philip, Bloomsbury, 1991.

Gordimer, Nadine (ed.). *Telling Tales*. London: Bloomsbury, 2004.

Gordimer, Nadine. *The House Gun*. London: Bloomsbury, 1999. [first published 1998]

Gray, Stephen (ed.). *The Penguin Book of Southern African Stories*. Harmondsworth: Penguin, 1985.

Gray, Stephen (ed.). *The Penguin Book of Southern African Verse*. London: Penguin, 1989.

Gregg, Lyndall. *Memories of Olive Schreiner*. London and Edinburgh: W. & R. Chambers Ltd, 1957.

Hallett, Robin. *Africa Since 1875*. University of Michigan Press, 1974.

Holland, Heidi and Adam Roberts (eds). *From Jo'burg to Jozi, Stories about Africa's Infamous City*. Johannesburg: Penguin Books, 2002.

Jackson, Kennell. *America Is Me*. New York: HarperCollins Publishers, 1996.

Jacobs, Rayda. *Post-Cards from South Africa*, Cape Town:

Double Storey Books, 2004.

James, Adeola (ed.). *In Their Own Voices: African Women Writers Talk*. London: Heinemann, 1990.

Johnson, Elisabeth. *Just Johannesburg*. Diep River: Chameleon Press, 1988.

Kaleeba, Noerine with Sunanda Ray and Brigid Willmore. *We Miss You All, Noerine Kaleeba: AIDS in the Family*. Harare, Zimbabwe: Woman and AIDS Support Network (WASN), 1991.

Kaleeba, Noerine, with Sunanda Ray. *We Miss You All; Noerine Kaleeba: AIDS in the Family*. Zimbabwe: SafAIDS, second edition, 2002.

Kaplan, Justin (ed.). *Bartlett's Familiar Quotations, 16th Edition*. Boston: Little, Brown and Company, 1992.

Karnga, Abba. *Bassa Proverbs for Preaching and Teaching*. Accra, Ghana: Asempa Publishers, Christian Council of Ghana, 1996.

Karodia, Farida. *A Shattering of Silence*. Oxford: Heinemann, 1993.

Krog, Antjie. *A Change of Tongue*. Johannesburg: Random House, 2003.

Kudadjie, Joshua N. *Ga and Dangme Proverbs for Preaching and Teaching*. Accra, Ghana: Asempa Publishers, Christian Council of Ghana, 1996.

Lennox-Short, Alan and Brian S Lee. *A Treasury of Quotations*. South Africa: AD Donker, 1991.

Lessing, Doris. *The Story of a Non-Marrying Man and Other Stories*. London: Paladin Books, 1990. [first published 1972]

Oufkir, Malika. *Stolen Lives, Twenty Years in a Desert Jail*. New York: Hyperion, 1999.

Maja-Pearce, Adewale. *The Heinemann Book of African Poetry in English*. London: Heinemann, 1990.

Makeba, Miriam, with James Hall. *Makeba, My Story*. New York: New American Library, 1988.

Mandela Zindzi. *Black as I am*. Los Angeles: Guild of Tutors Press, 1978.

Mapanje, Jack and Landeg White. *Oral Poetry from Africa, An Anthology*. UK: Longman Group, 1983.

Markham, Beryl. *West With the Night*. London: Penguin Books, 1988. [first published 1942]

Mashinini, Emma. *Strikes Have Followed Me All My Life*. New York: Routledge, 1991. [first published 1989]

Matthee, Dalene. *The Day the Swallows Spoke*. London: Penguin Books, 1992.

Mazrui, Ali A. *The Africans: A Triple Heritage*. Boston: Little, Brown and Company, 1986.

McKnight, Reginald (ed.). *Wisdom of the African World*. Novato, CA: New World Library, 1996.

Medalie, David (ed.). *Encounters, An Anthology of South African Short Stories*. Johannesburg: Witwatersrand University Press, 1998.

Mphande, David K. *Tonga Proverbs from Malawi: Proverbs for Preaching and Teaching Series*. Zomba, Malawi: 2001.

Packer, Joy. *Valley of the Vines*. London: Eyre & Spottiswoode, 1955.

Partnow, Elaine. *The Quotable Woman, Volume Two 1900-Present*. Los Angeles: Pinnacle Books, 1977.

Partnow, Elaine. *The New Quotable Woman*. New York: Facts on File, 1992.

Penguin Books. *Great South Africans, The Great Debate*. Johannesburg: Penguin Books, 2004.

Petras, Kathryn and Ross (comp. and ed.). *Whole World Book of Quotations: Wisdom from Women and Men Around the Globe Throughout the Centuries*. Reading, Massachusetts: Addison Wesley, 1995.

Piersen, William D. *From Africa to America*. New York: Twayne Publishers, 1996.

Reed, John and Clive Wake. *A New Book of African Verse*. London: Heinemann, 1984.

Ruete, Emily. *Memoirs of an Arabian Princess from Zanzibar*. New York: Marcus Wiener, 1989.

Russell, Diana E H. *Lives of Courage: Women for a New South Africa*. New York: Basic Books, 1989.

Sadat, Jehan. *A Woman of Egypt*. New York: Simon and Schuster, 1987.

Said, Laila. *A Bridge Through Time: A Memoir*. New York: Summit Books, 1985.

Scanlon, Paul A (ed.). *Stories from Central and Southern Africa*. London: Heinemann, 1983.

Schoeman, Karl. *Only an Anguish to Live Here, Olive Schreiner and the Anglo-Boer War 1899-1902*. Cape Town and Johannesburg: Human & Rousseau, 1992.

Schreiner, Barbara (ed.). *A Snake With Ice Water, Prison Writings by South African Women*. Johannesburg: Congress of South African Writers (COSAW), 1992.

Schreiner, Olive. *The Story of An African Farm*. London: Penguin Books, 1995. [first published 1883]

Schreiner, Olive. *Thoughts on South Africa*. Parklands: AD. Donker, 1992. [first published 1923]

Schreiner, Olive. *Thoughts on South Africa*. Johannesburg: Africana Book Society, 1976 reprint. [first published 1923]

Schreiner, Olive. *Woman and Labour*. London: Virago, 1978 reprint. [first published 1911]

Searle, Chris. *We're Building a New School, Diary of a Teacher in Mozambique*. London: Zed Press, 1981.

Sharp, Saundra. *Black Women for Beginners*. New York: Writers and Readers, 1993.

Smith, Pauline. *The Little Karoo*. Jonathan Cape, 1951 reprint. [first published 1925]

Smithers, Elsa. *March Hare, The Autobiography of Elsa Smithers*. London: Oxford University Press, 1935.

South African P.E.N. Centre. *New South African Writing*. Cape Town: Purnell & Sons, 1964.

Strathern, Oona. *Traveler's Literary Companion: Africa*. Illinois: Passport Books, 1995.

Suttner, Immanuel. *Cutting Through the Mountain, Interviews with South African Jewish Activists*. Johannesburg: Viking, 1997.

Tearle, Ruth. *Ride the Wild Tiger*. ComPress: 2000.

Thamm, Marianne and Toby Newsome. *The How-to-Be a South African Handbook*. Cape Town: Double Storey, 2002.

Thamm, Marianne. *Mental Floss*. Claremont, South Africa: Spearhead, 2002.

Tlali, Miriam. *Muriel at Metropolitan*. Washington, D.C.: Three Continents Press, 1977.

Troupe, Quincy and Rainer Schulte (eds). *Giant Talk, An Anthology of Third World Writings*. New York: Random House, 1975.

Van der Laan, Annelise (ed.). *Woman's Forum*. Pretoria: Daan Retief Publishers.

Zwi, Rose. *Another Year in Africa*. Johannesburg: Bateleur Press, 1980.

Speaker index

Sudanese Catholic saint: *43, 157, 176*

Bangura, Zainab Hawa (1959-) Sierra Leonean activist and politician: *174, 199*

Bauer, Charlotte (contemporary) South African journalist: *103, 211*

Bedj, Fatma (20th century) Algerian woman who lost three children in the fight for independence: *51-52*

Benga, Sokhna (contemporary) Senegalese scriptwriter and novelist: *38, 73*

Beyala, Calixthe (1961-) Cameroonian novelist: *4, 26, 45, 62, 78, 94, 95, 99, 113, 137, 145, 172*

Block, Donna (contemporary) South African journalist: *81*

Bonetti, Mahen (contemporary) cinema curator from Sierra Leone: *4, 6, 28-29, 38-39*

Boof, Kola [born Naima Bint Harith] (1969) 'Sudan's Eva Peron', Sudanese-American writer and activist: *1, 18-19, 20, 44, 57, 79, 102-103, 112, 125, 156, 170, 175, 194-195, 196, 209*

Boubacar, Mariama (contemporary) farmer from Niger: *203*

Bugul, Ken [pen name of Mariétou Bileoma M'Baye] (1948-) Senegalese writer: *12, 44, 55, 76-77*

Busia, Abena P A (1953-) Ghanaian poet, daughter of Dr Kofi Busia: *62, 129*

Byanyima, Winnie (contemporary) Ugandan politician: *60*

Camp, Sokari Douglas (1958-) Nigerian sculptress: *17*

Casely-Hayford, Gladys May (aka Aquah Laluah) (1904-1950) Ghanaian-born poet and teacher in Sierra Leone, daughter of J E and Adelaide: *51, 98, 129*

Chigudu, Hope (contemporary) Zimbabwean activist: *197*

Chirwa, Vera (contemporary) Malawian lawyer and human rights activist: *148*

Clayton, Cherry (1943-) South African writer: *147*

Coyne, Fiona (contemporary) South African playwright and television presenter: *4*

d'Almeida, Irène Assiba (contemporary) poet, translator, and professor from Benin: *147*

Dangarembga, Tsitsi (1969-) Zimbabwean writer: *7, 19, 32-33, 39, 88, 108-109, 127, 152, 173, 210*

Fugard, Sheila (1932-) South African novelist and poet, married to Athol Fugard: *5, 8, 22, 63, 64, 85, 89, 154, 177, 190, 208*

Fuller, Alexandra (1969-) British journalist and writer, raised in Zimbabwe: *42, 75, 106-107, 214*

Gabi, Ruth (1954-) Zimbabwean writer and teacher: *66*

Gashe, Marina [Rebecca Njau] (1932) Kenyan playwright, novelist and teacher: *207*

Gbedo, Marie-Elise Akouavi (contemporary) Beninois lawyer and first female presidential candidate: *149*

Ghomri, Halima (20th century) woman fighter in the Algerian war of independence against France: *52*

Ginwala, Frene (1932-) South African anti-apartheid activist and politician: *47-48*

Gordimer, Nadine (1923-) South African writer: *10, 12, 14, 22, 25, 29-30, 32, 45, 53-54, 67, 81, 85, 88-89, 128, 129-130, 134, 136, 154, 174, 177, 185, 196, 201, 206*

Gregg, Lyndall (20th century) niece of South African writer Olive Schreiner: *104-105, 119, 211*

Hadiza, Issa (contemporary) farmer from Niger: *40-41*

Hatshepsut, Queen (*c*.1540– *c*.1481 BC) Egyptian queen of the Eighteenth Dynasty, dressed as a man and crowned herself king: *166*

Hawoldar, Shakuntala (1944-) Indian-born poet living in Mauritius: *117, 135*

Head, Bessie Emery (1937-1986) South African-born Botswanan writer: *15, 24, 55, 63-64, 117, 145-146, 151, 165, 169*

Hendrikz, Annemarie (contemporary) South African activist: *162*

Heyns, Penny (1974-) South African breaststroke swimmer: *49*

Hocine, Baya (*b.c*.1940) Algerian journalist and independence fighter: *172*

Holland, Heidi (contemporary) South African journalist and writer: *11, 36*

Iman (Iman Mohamed Abdulmajid) (1955-) Somali-born supermodel: *51*

Imoukhuede, Mabel *see* Segun, Mabel

Isaacson, Maureen (1955-) South African writer and journalist: *99, 183*

Mashinini, Emma (1929-) South African trade unionist: *15, 162*

Matthee, Dalene (1938-2005) South African novelist: *7, 36, 49, 62, 79, 82, 85-86, 89, 106, 127, 155, 180, 181, 193*

McFadden, Patricia (1952-) scholar and feminist from Swaziland: *169*

Meer, Fatima (1928-) South African liberation struggle leader and writer: *39*

Mhlope, Gcina (1959-) South African writer and actress: *32, 88*

Millin, Sarah Gertrude (1889-1968) South African writer: *84, 166*

Mokhele, Elizabeth (contemporary) South African activist: *161*

Mompati, Ruth (1925-) South African anti-apartheid activist and ANC official: *137, 144*

Moss, Rose Rappoport (1937-) South African author and academic: *194*

Moussa, Sameera (1917-1952) Egyptian nuclear research scientist: *167*

Muchimba, Helen (contemporary) Zambian-based journalist: *28, 214*

Mugo, Micere Githae (1942-) Kenyan poet, critic and playwright: *41, 114*

Muholi, Zanele (contemporary) South African artist: *16*

Mukagasana, Yolande (1954-) Rwandan nurse and human rights advocate: *32*

Mumba, Samantha (1983-) Zambian-Irish pop star: *11*

Ngcobo, Gabi (1974-) South African artist: *86*

Ngcobo, Lauretta (1931-) South African writer: *167, 172*

Ngilu, Charity (1952-) Kenyan politician: *148*

Nongqause (19th century) Xhosa prophet: *30*

Noot (ancient Egypt) god of the sky: *112*

Nujoma, Kovambo (contemporary) wife of president Sam Nujoma of Namibia: *95*

Nwapa, Flora (1931-1993) Nigerian novelist: *134*

Nyeck, Sybille Ngo (contemporary) Cameroonian columnist: *170*

Odundo, Magdalene (1950-) Kenyan potter: *17*

Ogot, Grace Emily Akinyi (1930-) Kenyan writer: *43*

Ogundipe-Leslie, Molara (1949-)

Nigerian poet and academic: *79*

Okoye, Ifeoma (contemporary)
Nigerian novelist, children's
writer, and lecturer: *125*

O'Lahsen, Malika (1930-)
Algerian poet: *57*

Olembu, Norah (contemporary)
Kenyan scientist: *65*

Oludhe Macgoye, Marjorie
(1928-) English-born, natural-
ised Kenyan missionary book-
seller, writer and poet: *34, 135,
147, 207*

Onwueme, Tess Onsonye
(1955-) Nigerian playwright:
2, 178

Orakwue, Stella (contemporary)
Nigerian journalist: *103, 107*

Oriang, Lucy (contemporary)
Kenyan journalist and editor:
110

Oufkir, Malika (1953-)
Moroccan heiress, imprisoned
for 20 years: *57, 98-99*

Ovbiagele, Helen (1944-)
Nigerian writer and editor:
84, 109

Packer, Joy (1905-1977) South
African novelist: *135, 138, 181,
185-186*

Perlman, Ina (1926-) South
African activist: *68, 96*

Perry, Ruth Sando (1939-)

Liberian teacher, banking
executive, and politician, was
Chair of the Council of State
from 1996-1997, making her
the first female African head of
state: *26, 154-155, 199*

Phalane, Payne (contemporary)
South African artist: *16*

Phetlhu, Shollo (contemporary)
Botswanan media executive:
123

Pillay, Maganthrie (1971-)
South African filmmaker: *16,
27, 149, 205*

Podbrey, Pauline (1922-) South
African trade unionist: *104*

Quachey, Lucia (contemporary)
Ghanaian entrepreneur: *112*

Queen of Sheba (*see* Makeda)

Ramgobin, Ela (1941-) South
African anti-apartheid
activist and granddaughter of
Mahatma Gandhi: *121*

Ramphele, Mamphela (1947-)
South African doctor and
academic: *33*

Rasoanaivo, Hanitra (contemporary) Malagasy musician:
34, 61, 116, 151, 165, 171-172

Rawlings, Nana Konadu (1948-)
wife of Jerry Rawlings, former
president of Ghana: *144*

Redfern-Duff, Yvonne (contemporary) South African

limerick contest winner: *214*

Reitstein, Amy (1932-) South African activist: *144-145*

Roberts, Sheila (1937-) South African writer: *53, 104*

Romm, Nina (1949-) South African artist: *207*

Rungano, Kristina (1963-) poet and computer scientist from Zimbabwe: *214*

Saadawi, Nawal El (1931-) Egyptian writer, psychiatrist and feminist: *12, 23, 50, 69-70, 78, 80, 87, 94, 96, 105, 108, 118, 123-124, 135, 142, 146-147, 152, 159, 160-161, 164, 167, 188-189, 198, 205, 213*

Sacks, Caroline (contemporary) South African journalist: *127*

Sadat, Jehan (1933?-) wife of Egyptian president Anwar Sadat: *57*

Sade [born Helen Folasade Adu] (1959-) Nigerian singer: *40, 114*

Said, Laila (1941-) Egyptian writer: *115*

Sampson, Lin (contemporary) South African journalist: *181*

Sandasi, M (contemporary) Zimbabwean poet: *203*

Santo, Alda do Espírito (1926-) educator and poet from São Tomé e Príncipe: *176*

Schreiner, Olive, [pseudonym Ralph Iron] (1855-1920) South African writer, feminist, and pacifist: *1, 3, 6, 8, 9, 11, 18, 20, 21, 24, 25, 33, 34, 35, 39-40, 43, 44, 45, 48, 49, 58, 59-60, 64-65, 67, 70, 75, 77, 80, 81, 82, 85, 88, 90, 94, 97, 98, 101, 106, 116, 117, 120, 122-123, 126, 128, 130, 132, 138, 140, 141, 147, 148, 150, 152, 153, 155, 157, 168, 169, 173, 178, 179, 180-181, 184, 186, 187-188, 190-191, 193-194, 201, 202, 203, 204, 206, 208, 211, 214*

Segun, Mabel (1930-) Nigerian poet and educator: *100, 150*

September, Dulcie (1953-1988) South African writer and political activist, killed by a bomb in her office: *14*

Shafik, Dorreya (1908-) Egyptian women's rights activist: *46*

Sheba, Queen of Ethiopia (*see* Makeda)

Sherry, Shannon (contemporary) South African journalist: *56*

Shoneyin, Lola (1974-) Nigerian poet and editor: *16, 22, 37, 74, 110, 120-121, 123, 124, 133, 170, 212*

Sikakane, Joyce Nomafa (1943-) South African poet, writer, and anti-apartheid campaigner: *31*

Siré, Mahabara (contemporary) farmer from Burkina Faso: *204*